How to Master the Inner Game of Golf

How to Master the Inner Game of Golf

MAXINE VAN EVERA LUPO

Illustrations by Dom Lupo

TAYLOR TRADE PUBLISHING
Lanham • New York • Boulder • Toronto • Plymouth, UK

Published by Taylor Trade Publishing
An imprint of The Rowman & Littlefield Publishing Group, Inc.
4501 Forbes Boulevard, Suite 200, Lanham, Maryland 20706
www.rlpgtrade.com

Estover Road, Plymouth PL6 7PY, United Kingdom

Distributed by NATIONAL BOOK NETWORK

Library of Congress Cataloging-in-Publication Data

Lupo, Maxine Van Evera, 1921-
    How to master the inner game of golf / Maxine Van Evera Lupo ; Illustrations by Dom Lupo.
        p. cm.
    Includes index.
    ISBN-13: 978-1-58979-416-0 (pbk. : alk. paper)
    ISBN-10: 1-58979-416-8 (pbk. : alk. paper)
    ISBN-13: 978-1-58979-417-7 (electronic)
    ISBN-10: 1-58979-417-6 (electronic)
    1. Golf—Psychological aspects. 2. Golf—Training. I. Lupo, Dom. II. Title.
GV979.P75L87 2009
796.352—dc22   2009000689

∞™ The paper used in this publication meets the minimum requirements of American National Standard for Information Sciences—Permanence of Paper for Printed Library Materials, ANSI/NISO Z39.48-1992.

Manufactured in the United States of America.

Contents

CONTENTS

Introduction and Acknowledgments

Written as a supplement to my first book, *How to Master a Great Golf Swing*, *How to Master the Inner Game of Golf* was written as a motivational book with emphasis on how golfers themselves contribute to and impact the game they already are playing.

Understanding oneself, as well as understanding the game of golf, is essential to playing with confidence and proficiency, often even resulting in the awesome, yet unexplainable experience of having played "in the zone"—a round of golf where someone played far beyond even their own expectations. In my opinion, golfers who experience this rare phenomenon, regardless of their level of proficiency, inadvertently will have applied, at that particular moment in time, not only their own unique physical talent but also a summation of all of the knowledge found within these pages.

Learning is a lifelong dedication for dedicated golfers. For those who are not that dedicated as yet but who want to become more proficient, an index also is included to help you locate and apply the knowledge you will have assimilated.

Since no one is an entity unto themselves when it comes to assimilating knowledge, and although I owe much to many along the way, I have special appreciation for and owe thanks to many friends, critics, and writers throughout the years for their knowledgeable guidance, historical input, and support.

Going back a few years, many, many thanks to my longtime friend, Barbara Quinn, for her literary help and enduring patience, as well as to a special friend and neighbor, 1940 USGA amateur champion Richard (Dick) Chapman, now deceased, who first encouraged me; to Nancy Crossman who promoted my first publication; to PGA professionals Eddie Merrins, Jim Porter, and Don Collett; as well as to former UCLA golf coach, Dr. Ray Snyder; all of whom, from the beginning, believed in what I was doing.

Also, many thanks more recently to Clem Hale, USGA Committee Member; to Sports Psychologist Dr. Jay Brunza, who again "kept me out of harm's way"; and to my friend and computer-literate neighbor, Rex Shepherd, who occasionally saved the day; also to Peter Burford, and our publishers who initiated this publication; and certainly to my husband, Dom, for his support and wonderful illustrations that enhance yet another of his many books.

And, finally, but certainly not the least, thanks to all of our many readers whose letters of appreciation for our first book encouraged us both to collaborate yet again on helping golfers help themselves.

PART I

The Challenge

CHAPTER ONE

Why Golf Is Such a Challenge

Golf in its simplest form is defined as "a leisure activity performed for enjoyment in competition against someone." Although not always "a leisure activity" in that it commonly causes stress, anxiety, and frustration, there are two kinds of competition. The first is where either (1) they win and you lose because they beat you, or else (2) you win and they lose because you beat them. The second, though, is where they win and you lose because you beat yourself. Probably the greatest challenge in golf, therefore, is learning how not to beat yourself.

As a youngster, Bobby Jones once said he thought golf was "just a game to beat someone," but added, "I didn't know the someone was myself." He soon became a student of the game, regarded competition as a challenge, and subsequently became not only a great player but also a great writer and teacher as well.

Understandably, since it takes time and dedication to become a proficient golfer, as opposed to becoming just another player, not everyone is destined to become proficient; nor is everyone even desirous of trying. On the other hand, there are millions of players worldwide who want to improve and who want to win who just keep beating themselves.

We all fall prey to losing by beating ourselves when we fail to realize three things: First, most problems in golf are caused by a poor golf swing. Second, you must be mentally sharp enough and emotionally strong enough to withstand the pressure of competition. Third, you must be physically prepared to compete on an equal level with your opponent. Oddly enough, even learning something about the history of golf is a step toward self-improvement. For instance, recorded history from the early fifteenth century indicates that golf evolved from "hearty men finding recreation with a stick and ball on the sandy dunes and coastal shores of Scotland." Also recorded in that era were drawings showing players swinging and hitting a "featherie" with a hickory stick by turning the body and shifting the weight with natural swinging and hitting movements. And so it is today, although there still remains a certain knack required for doing so with accuracy and proficiency.

In preparation for swinging and hitting, muscles anticipate such action and prepare themselves accordingly, thereby providing the very foundation for the golf swing. To feel this natural action, first get set to throw a ball sidearm-underhand with just one hand down an imaginary target line. Now simply draw back and throw the ball (either real or imaginary) down that line (Illustration 1.1). Although swing movements are all fairly natural with one hand, rarely is it understood that the movement quickly becomes more difficult, more *un*natural, and more challenging when both hands do this together—as in golf.

Because of this unnatural requirement for golf—where the body turns rotationally and the arms swing upward with the hands together—through the years fundamental guidelines have evolved for certain basic positions at address that promote hitting the ball both far and straight, whereas shots other than straight result from simply changing these positions. In turn, however, changing any of these "basics," either intentionally—or more often

1.1   You can do this, too. It's just harder with both hands together.

*un*intentionally—also changes swing movement, thereby changing the results. Hence the value of understanding the golf swing and essential positions as a whole.

Learning how to play golf first uses conscious thought to develop the physical part of golf until the golf swing develops into subconscious action through practicing correct positions and swing movements. Once an accurate swing is established and no longer requires total awareness, conscious thought can then be redirected from the physical aspect of golf to the mental.

Although golf combines one's physical and emotional capability with its own provocative nature, players also permeate their entire golf game with their own personality traits as they deal with both conscious and subconscious behavior. Aside from perhaps not having a sound golf swing, they encounter difficulty by not understanding how they themselves impact their own golf game with their own emotional makeup. They fail to recognize that it may not be the course, the weather, other players, or supernatural forces causing problems, but oftentimes their own destructive attitude and temperament that they fail to recognize and overcome. In 1973, golf journalist Peter Dobereiner wrote in his book, *The Glorious World of Golf,*

> Many a golfer has been destroyed more by his own sensitivity than by the course or his opponent. But it is a matter of simple observation that the very best players are highly intelligent men who recognize the demons conjured up in their own imagination and face them squarely for what they are. The unimaginative clod with a sound method can make a good golfer, but it takes brains to make a great one.

Although much has been written about teaching and learning golf, meeting the challenge of playing well still comes from within ourselves—what we learn and how well we apply that to playing. In other words, we steadily improve in golf not by how much we already know but how much we continue to learn and apply it. Those who apply this practice are those who understand the problems and continue to meet the challenges. And that's what makes golfers individuals with golf games so diverse.

What most golfers need, therefore, is not to give up the game or to continue to play poorly, but to apply a greater effort toward meeting the challenge of learning. Knowledge, understanding, application, and practice help eliminate frustration, thereby making golf more of a challenge by making it less complex.

CHAPTER TWO

Meeting the Challenge

Once described as "a revealing form of self-expression, exposing us to others for who and what we are," golf remains a challenging way of life unlike any other. Continually testing our mental and physical prowess and our ability to control our emotions as we act and react, the game brings pleasure beyond belief to those who recognize and meet its challenges.

Because of the seemingly complex nature of golf, instruction through the ages has encompassed everything from Scottish caddies helping their players through the gorse and heather to the current use of sports psychology. Through the years, however, there still remain the multitudes who are unable to play well simply because they have no guidelines. Without guidelines, though, players seldom develop their own potential.

They simply start playing, often quite badly, and continue to play with frustration resulting from an inability to hit the ball well and not knowing what to do or how to go about it.

Although players accept all this and still pursue the game, the problem remains that too many people give up the game, too many play poorly, and too many subscribe to the belief that "that's just the way it is." Since golf is a way of life unlike any other for those who understand and meet its challenges, however, that's neither the way it needs to be nor should be. Improvement starts by learning about the mental as well about the physical aspects of the game of golf.

To become a proficient golfer and meet the challenge of playing well you must be knowledgeable, not only about requirements for the golf swing itself that provide guidelines for playing, but also about yourself and how you impact your own golf game.

Your feelings and emotions, even your character, affect your whole golf game by how you perform, how you act toward others, how you think about things, and how you deal with your strengths and weaknesses. Even as we become more knowledgeable, though, it seems that the more we think, the worse we play. Is it possible then that the two sides of golf, the physical and the mental, are not really compatible when it comes to playing golf? No, certainly not. One encompasses the other. To blend the two, however, you need to understand the golf swing, and you need to understand how you influence both the mental and physical components of golf.

One should never underestimate golf as just a game of "hit the ball, find it, hit it again." *Au contraire.* The challenge of golf is to accurately hit the woods and irons with power and control while pitching, chipping, and putting with finesse and "feel." To do this, you need to learn what is required, then implement in practice the correct, mechanical procedure until it becomes subconscious action. Don't be discouraged, though, as you accept the challenge. The enjoyment of playing golf continually increases as you improve your own performance.

Until you gain proficiency, you run the gamut of emotions in golf as you deal with both success and failure, both of which are present anytime, anywhere. You are continually barraged by both conscious and subconscious behavior that often causes problems. Only when you know what causes problems can you prevent them, though, and only when you recognize when you have one are you able to correct it. Dealing with either prevention or correction totally involves the mental as well as the physical aspect of golf. To attain a higher level of proficiency it really is imperative that you understand both aspects.

Much of what we first learn about golf we seem to garner by osmosis. To steadily improve in golf, however, requires understanding basic, fundamental positions and movements as well as learning how they all work together within our own physical ability. The challenge then is to further improve the physical aspect of your game by also improving your mental ability.

Those who successfully engage in this advanced form of thinking and playing have long since developed their strengths and overcome their weaknesses, which most players have yet to accomplish. After years of application and practice, the mind and body of a highly proficient golfer are not at odds with each other. They've become completely simpatico. Touring professionals, for instance, who certainly understand and apply basics, have many times over encountered and had to deal with their own personal traits and tendencies, overcoming some while using others as stepping-stones to proficiency. They play the game exceedingly well by having turned knowledge of the game and of themselves into two important assets: (1) the subconscious application of mechanics, and (2) concentration on making the golf shot at hand.

Learning how to swing, or perhaps learning how to improve or correct a golf swing, is accomplished by either taking lessons from an accredited Professional Golfers Association (PGA) or Ladies Professional Golf Association (LPGA) teaching professional or by using any proven self-help instructional book that explains and helps you understand the many facets of golf. Although self-help with the use of a good instructional book is an acceptable method for learning, learning about golf as taught by teachers who teach and explain the importance of time-proven basics is undoubtedly the most expedient and gratifying method for both learning and improving personal performance. A good instructional book will then be useful by helping you recognize and deal with your own problem areas. Whatever your method, however, equally as important as learning about the physical aspect of golf is learning about the mental aspect of golf that helps you understand and deal with your ability, attitude, personality, emotions, and character, as well as with your concentration and confidence.

With practice, the margin of difference continually narrows between physical and mental prowess, moving the two closer and closer together until one embraces the other. However, do not make the mistake of thinking that this is accomplished either permanently or instantaneously with one good book, a series of lessons, and a few quick trips to the driving range. It takes several years for a player to become a bona fide golfer as opposed to becoming just another player. As you accept the challenge, though, remember that, regardless of method or technique, you *will* increase the enjoyment of playing as you improve your own performance.

As golfers develop their own golf game, the mental aspect of golf impacts thinking in different ways. Whereas experienced golfers may apply thinking to an advanced form of shotmaking—the art of "shaping" golf shots either over, under, or around trees or "doglegs," for instance— less experienced golfers apply thinking to simply swinging and hitting the golf ball. Although both require thinking and planning about how and where to play the shot, *every* shot also involves the mental aspect of golf that requires both concentration and confidence that directly influence results.

Since the hardest shot of all to hit consistently well for most golfers is a "dead straight" ball over a bunker, under a tree, or over water, for instance, simply making the shot to the best of one's ability should, initially at least, be the goal of most players. Therefore, players should not stress the importance of becoming a "shotmaker," per se, but should stress improving both concentration and confidence. And how is this done? It's done through knowledge and by practicing time-proven basics.

The game of golf makes demands and dictates conformity, but part of its fascination, and certainly the challenge, is learning how to find and use the tools that help you overcome the problems in your own golf game. As the saying goes, "It's not the problem but how you deal with it that counts." Eventually, as you learn the purpose and importance of positions and essential swing movements, you will be able to recognize if, when, and where you need help, and you will know how and where to find it. And therein lies the secret to meeting the challenge in golf.

Along with the challenge of learning how to win by learning how not to beat ourselves is the challenge of accepting the frustration until we overcome the problems.

PART II

Self-Help

CHAPTER THREE

Methods for Self-Help

Through the years even the best of players have been challenged by anger and poor concentration, and have had to seek solutions. Small wonder, then, that to improve in golf you have to come to grips with exactly who's at fault, who is in charge, and accept self-help as the answer. Self-help in golf is not just being self-taught and playing forever with whatever the result may be. It means having the ability to determine where you are, where you're going, what you need to get there, and then take action in a positive direction. By understanding yourself as well as by understanding the basic golf swing, and by learning what else is available to help you, soon you are able to assess your strengths and weaknesses, play better, and enjoy the game more by deciding the tack you want to take to improve your own performance.

Whatever your level of expertise, implementing self-help as a useful tool in golf will improve your game considerably as you overcome stress and frustration with knowledge and ability. But nobody can help you as well as you can help yourself because problems start between the ears. So, to be an accomplished golfer you can't just learn to hit the ball; you have to learn to think. According to Jack Nicklaus, "Your mind is your strongest competitive weapon and by using your mind you're giving your game your best effort."

Let's consider the resources available for self-help in golf: When you arrive at the clubhouse for another exciting adventure on the golf course, for instance, how's your self-esteem? Do you know that first-tee self-esteem is enhanced by polished shoes, clean clubs, and appropriate golf attire? And not to be excluded as a factor in performance is arriving at the course ahead of time in a leisurely manner and pleasant frame of mind. All of these factors require planning, time, and patience to put it into application.

Improvement in golf also stems from learning about things we may not have thought about. Knowing the history of golf, for instance, enhances one's appreciation; understanding course management improves both thinking and strategy; and learning how to recognize and deal with golf-swing problems improves self-confidence. All of these contribute to two rewarding goals in golf: self-esteem in competition and enjoyment of the game.

Depending on desire, goals, and the current level of proficiency, the needs of individuals differ considerably in golf. Children, for instance, often start with only hand-me-down golf clubs (and hopefully someone knowledgeable enough about basics to occasionally help them), whereas touring professionals have state-of-the-art equipment and often a knowledgeable retainer (e.g., a teacher, coach, or sports psychologist) who knows their swing, understands basics, and regularly checks their swing for accuracy.

By far the majority of golfers, though, are neither beginners nor professionals. They are average golfers just like you, perhaps, who may or may not have had either lessons or adequate equipment, but who definitely want to improve.

Options available for improvement in golf are threefold: (1) Seek professional help; (2) improve and expand your knowledge to better employ self-help; or (3) use a combination of both—the latter being preferred.

YOU AND YOUR OPTIONS

Upgrading your golf game is best undertaken with help from others who are trained in the field. Although there always will be someone only too glad to help you, it's distinctly to your advantage if they understand the golf swing—and few volunteers are qualified. On the other hand, a qualified teacher who understands basics can definitely help you with your golf swing as well as help you understand it. Such is the value of professionalism.

Aside from qualified outside help, self-help still remains an important factor in improvement because you are the one who makes decisions and choices about where you are, where you want to be, and what you're willing or able to do to get there based on desire and results. However, when making decisions to improve your game either by improving your swing or upgrading your golf equipment, one thing is certain: No matter how good the equipment, it can never be a substitute for a sound golf swing.

Lessons and Equipment

When first learning golf, too many golfers try to fit a flawed golf swing to happenstance equipment, which leads to compensation and faulty swing habits. Once you've mastered swing mechanics, though, and have a sound golf swing, it's time to maximize your own efficiency by testing golf equipment well-suited for your use. So many factors are involved, however, that in order to select intelligently it's wise to seek professional help.

Teaching professionals who are members of either the PGA or LPGA are exceptionally well-qualified to help golfers at every level of expertise who are looking for improvement. Many years of schooling and training are required to become a teaching professional. Once accredited, they and their assistants may be found at golf facilities worldwide where they offer private and group lessons, golf schools, special clinics, help with equipment, and direct both junior and senior programs.

The alternative to taking advantage of lessons given by a professional, of course, is for you to know how to help yourself. For those who choose to either learn or improve their game through a self-help program, several resources are available: (1) books and magazines; (2) visual aids; (3) observation; and, of course, (4) practice.

Books

Centuries-old and modern-day writings have recorded everything imaginable about the game of golf and have made books a treasured and invaluable source of information. Gifted writers teaming together with knowledgeable players in the writing of books have many times over become the vanguard for a player's proficiency; so, in conjunction with your interest, ability, and intelligence, self-help in golf can be accomplished to varying degrees with persistence, dedication, and a good golf book.

As golf becomes more of a science, new books by new writers, oftentimes collaborating with well-established players, continue to promote the program. But in searching out the new books, don't forget the old. Golf instruction is, and always has been, based on the natural ability of various parts of the body to coordinate in a swinging-hitting action. Since the structure of the body has not changed over the years, neither have the basics; therefore, when considering the use of helpful golf books, remember that the earlier instructional books are also very helpful in a self-help program. The value of such golf books is measured by collections throughout the world, one of which belongs to the United States Golf Association (USGA) at their Golf House in Far Hills, New Jersey.

Golf House, open to the public, is an elegant and beautifully cared-for Georgian colonial mansion (Illustration 3.1) displaying several centuries of artifacts and golf memorabilia. Also housed within is a library of more than ten thousand books on golf. Regarded as one of the largest collections, this resource is available to researchers seeking data on everything conceivable in golf from the earliest times. Many volumes are irreplaceable classics and first editions duplicating treasured copies also found in libraries and private collections throughout the world. The largest percentage of these are instructional books, but those on the history of golf are second in number, which certainly would pique your interest.

As noted by Bobby Jones in his foreword to a book by Charles Price, *The World of Golf,* "The lore of the game, the story of its development and of the stirring deeds of past great players always command the

3.1   USGA Golf House, Far Hills, New Jersey.

respectful attention of all who regularly play golf. To become reasonably knowledgeable about such matters seems close to being an obligation of the true golfer."

It generally is conceded by historians and known by golfers that golf first started on "the links"—a strip of sand dunes along a beach in Scotland—and that in the year 1457 King James II of Scotland proclaimed the game of golf to be illegal and determined that golf was no longer acceptable since it interfered with archery practice and thus adversely affected the army's readiness.

Although King James II's proclamation is noted as the first written reference to golf, the first published reference was a poem entitled "The Goff" written in 1743 by Thomas Mathison. Since these early references, though, several hundred years of writing have recorded all the enduring appeal and popularity of the game, as well as its methods and traditions. The creative works of golf's greatest writers showing concern, love, and passion for golf have been wonderfully expressed. As a golfer, whether a student of the game or not, how could it be possible to not avail yourself of all the many treasures found within these written pages?

Magazines

Along with golf-related articles and advertising for new equipment, golf schools, junior camps and programs, courses to play, travel, and so on, golf magazines also are a wonderful resource for instruction. Although they regularly feature exceptional articles by both players and teachers, where are these wonderful resources when you need them? Well, you can borrow the magazines back from the neighbor or dig them out of the trash, perhaps, or you can follow this suggestion: (1) Either buy or subscribe to at least one monthly golf magazine, and (2) learn to clip-and-file (Illustration 3.2).

Golf is a lifelong learning experience and magazines provide a wealth of information over time that is not only interesting at the moment, but also very accurate and extremely educational. Clipping articles and illustrations for reference purposes and filing them under subject headings helps you continually learn more and more about the golf swing while giving you quick and ready reference for comparison with your own. Illustrations and photos especially help you see and understand positions as well as sense the movement.

Consider the value of having a wealth of information in a reference file categorized in individual manila folders just for you provided by the best players, writers, teachers, illustrators, and photographers of both past and

3.2 Clippings provide a self-help reference file.

present decades. Consider the following example of a list of topics that might be included in a reference file on the backswing, for instance:

BACKSWING
Bobby Jones on
clubhead control in
fast
length of
pause at top of (See also: DOWNSWING, starting; TIMING)
preparation for
shortening
shoulder turn importance in
starting
weight shift importance in (See also: FOOTWORK; WEIGHT SHIFT)

Very little has changed or can be said about the golf swing that hasn't already been said or is different than before; hence the value of your file. Equipment may be a factor in improved performance, but problems that caused slicing 100 years ago with hickory shafts undoubtedly are the same problems that today cause slicing with graphite, steel, or titanium.

Any of several fairly common problems cause slicing, of course, so over time you may find you have filed several articles under the heading of slicing. Since everything old is made new again by writers saying the same thing differently for new readers, however, you'll find that filed subject matter may repeat itself at times. People learn in different ways, though, and we need new reminders about basics with a different slant on things from time to time.

There are those who will tell you that learning too much about the golf swing causes one to either become too analytical, too mechanical, or to focus only on what they're doing wrong. If that were true, and we shouldn't think too much or learn too much about the golf swing, then why are all the books and instructional articles written? Why all the lessons? Why all the teachers, gurus, trainers, coaches, and so on? Because players without interest in and dedication to learning continue to know only a little bit about a few things and not a lot about a lot of things, so they still are unable to either prevent or correct their problems.

Getting your own self-help file together takes time and effort—but then so does improving your golf game.

Visual Aids

Our faculties for learning golf are sight, sound, and touch; what we see, hear, and feel. We learn by observation, emulation, association, manipulation, participation, and even recreation; but we all learn differently because we use our senses differently. Regardless of how a player learns best, however, everyone should take advantage of the sense of sight by using visual aids.

Visual aids not only relate to books and magazines that include excellent photographs and illustrations. Observation and emulation include watching and doing what others do. For instance, (1) watching better golfers on a driving range, (2) watching teaching professionals give a lesson, (3) watching tournaments and golf instruction on television, and attending nearby tournaments to watch the tour players, and (4) using video instructional tapes and computer skills all are excellent for an in-depth study of a golf swing. Teaching professionals and golf schools routinely videotape students' golf swings for various reasons: It's easier for teachers to isolate a problem for close observation; it's easier for students to see flaws in their own swings than to feel it; and once students see the flaw, it's easier to make the changes necessary to correct it.

Professionals use these skills and tools most effectively and you can, too, to check your own performance. But do you know what to look for and do you recognize what you see? What are you leaving out of your swing—or incorrectly adding? You should know what your own golf swing looks like in order to use visual equipment effectively.

When you understand the golf swing you can compare every aspect of your own golf swing with basics. Videotape yourself both down target and straight on. Place a club along your feet to check alignment and use a background reference point, such as a tree, to check for body movement. You can check every position and movement from address to follow-through. Also helpful is comparing your own golf swing with photos and illustrations from your research file.

COURSE MANAGEMENT

Course management is the skillful art of staying out of trouble while working your way around a golf course. It is knowing how to play a golf course hole-by-hole with thoughtful planning, when to be aggressive, and how to be conservative.

Course management starts with knowing rules and knowing your strengths and weaknesses. Do you know how far you hit each club, for instance, and can you figure yardage? Can you open the clubface somewhat and "fly" a high golf shot? Which club? How high? Can you really play a sand wedge from a buried downhill bunker lie to a tight pin placement with a lake just beyond? Do you know that instead you can replay the last shot that put you there for only one additional stroke?

Recognizing your capabilities and knowing things in general such as rules and yardages give you confidence to play, all of which is only preparation for good course management where the key is strategy. Strategy is not just physical ability, but thoughtful preparation for each of the eighteen holes.

It is difficult to be efficient without composure; so, good or bad, forget your score on the previous hole entirely. If it was good you tend to slack off a bit and if it was bad you tighten up, either of which tends to influence both timing and concentration. You can't replay the last hole and you need your concentration to play the next one.

As you walk toward the next tee, first determine what is par, then study the fairway design. Search for hazards and problem areas so you can avoid trouble. Then, if possible, locate the green and pin placement. Before teeing up the ball, note the problem area. While the thought may be to tee the ball as far away from trouble as possible, this promotes hitting into trouble (Illustration 3.3; A). Unless you are extremely adept at curving the ball at will, the more prudent teeing area is on the same side as trouble in order to hit away from it (B).

Evaluating the trouble helps you define the target more clearly, giving you a more positive image of the shot you need to play. For instance, when there are fairway bunkers on the left and out of bounds on the right, hit it left. The penalty for a bunker shot is less severe than for hitting out of bounds.

Good course management initiates sensible game plans such as the following:

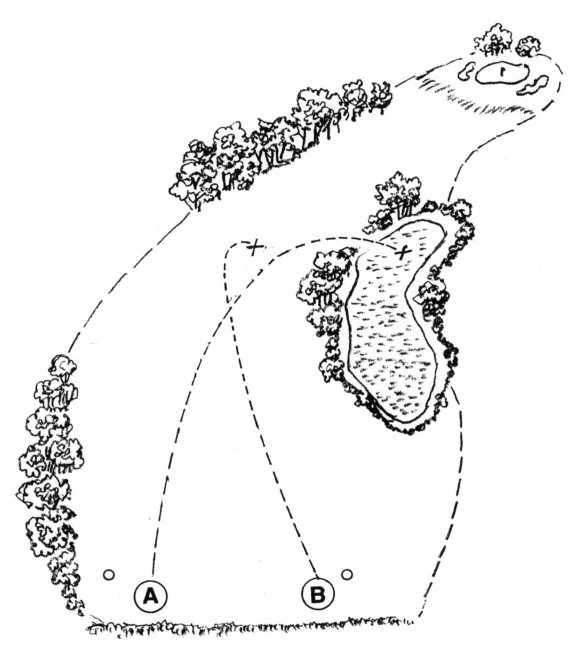

3.3 Good course management represents smart thinking.

Game Plan #1

Play conservatively when you're in trouble and play boldly when you're not. In other words, don't hit your driver out of the middle of a forest and don't lay up to a trouble-free green.

Game Plan #2

When you hit into trouble, don't even think about your next shot until you get there. Until then, relax. You can't plan options until you can assess your situation. No matter what the situation, course management requires staying composed in order to be consistent.

Game Plan #3

When you do hit into trouble on a par four hole, to avoid a double bogey forget making par and play the hole for a five. In the long run, playing for bogey may save a stroke or two.

Game Plan #4

Choose your target then trust your golf swing so you can first visualize, then concentrate only on making your golf shot.

VISUALIZATION

Visualization is being able to form a mental picture of something that is as yet invisible, in this case your next golf shot. As soon as you feel comfortable with positions and movements to the point where they become reliable, you should include visualization as part of your set-up procedure. This is important because your subconscious helps program your body for making the golf shot. In other words, positions and movements in a swinging-hitting action naturally try to coordinate to hit the ball toward an envisioned target.

But let's also be realistic. For instance, professional golfers can visualize a golf shot, then step up to the ball and hook it around to their envisioned target area (Illustration 3.4; A). Now although you may be able to hook the ball sometimes and can visualize the same shot somewhat, if you lack the expertise to intentionally make a golf shot that may be difficult for you, visualizing success is difficult and your body may not respond. Rather than "seeing" and focusing on the landing area, you see and focus on the golf ball as your target and simply swing with murderous intent.

Visualization reinforces your ability to make a golf shot. When you only think you might make it, however, and the shot is not critical at the moment to your winning or losing, you should visualize your safe shot which is easier to "see" (B). In this instance, it helps keep the ball out of trouble (C).

Being safe and accurate should be the first order of business for most golfers. But visualization isn't only for experts because they have the technical know-how; nor is it only for you when hitting safe shots. Visualization helps you overcome problems such as playing a particularly difficult hole where you lack confidence.

When you lack confidence, rather than worrying about it, visualize yourself playing your favorite golf hole where you consistently play well. Visualize your favorite landing area and bring it clearly into focus. The more decisively you can visualize, the more decisively you can aim and swing. In

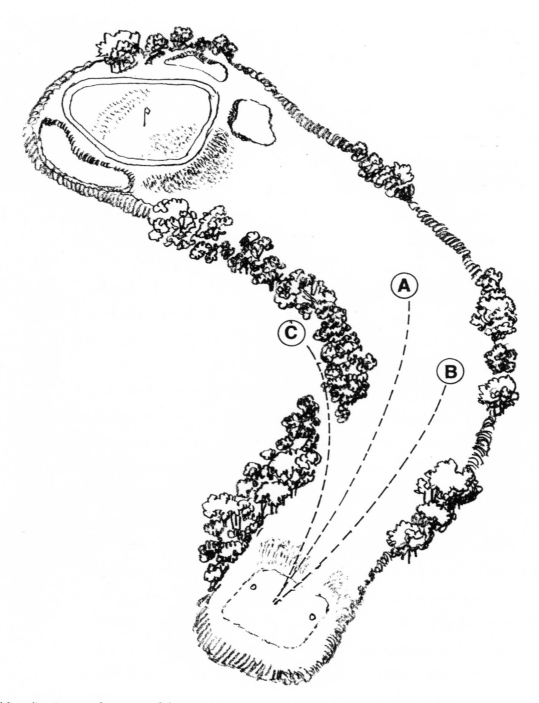

3.4 Visualization reinforces confidence.

another instance, when you have difficulty hitting over hazards, visualize a realistic landing area beyond the hazard (Illustration 3.5). Glance from the ball to the landing area a time or two, then focus on hitting the ball directly to that target. With practice you soon learn to see only the landing area.

Having a creative imagination is an important asset in golf, not to conjure up an image of doing the impossible but to reinforce your ability to do the possible.

PHYSICAL FITNESS

According to percentages, it has been said that ten percent of the populace support almost any program, whatever it is, ten percent reject it, and the eighty percent in the middle are neutral. In general then, should this be true, only ten percent of golfers subscribe to physical fitness, thereby probably placing the most dedicated golfers at the top of the ten-percent bracket.

Touring professionals in particular, from both the PGA and LPGA who pursue the high-level stakes of competition, almost collectively push themselves to the outer limits to hone their physical and mental abilities. Golf is their business—and helping *all* golfers play better, by the way, also is *big* business. Because of this, studying the golf swing in order to enhance proficiency has become such a science that performance is measured with sophisticated, hi-tech equipment. Computerized swing analyzers study physiological movement, how parts of the body work, and, within the spectrum of biomechanics, a process called electromyography studies how the muscles perform.

Studies involving top-level tour players have helped scientists define more clearly what the body needs to do to conform to golf swing

TARGET

3.5 Visualization really works!

movements. In return, players have learned what they need to do physically to improve their performance. The point is that golf professionals use everything available and every opportunity to improve their physical performance. Even though the difference may be that professionals play for many thousands—even millions—of dollars while you play for a trophy in your annual member-guest tournament, if you want to give a tournament your best effort, you also should consider physical fitness.

Improving physical fitness means conditioning your body in the areas of strength, flexibility, and health: strength with exercise, flexibility with drills, and health with diet and nutrition. Improving just one will improve your ability, but improving all three will improve your whole golf game by improving your attitude, disposition, and concentration, as well as your confidence and self-esteem.

Strength

Normal strength is maintained in everyday living by normal activity; and muscle building, per se, is not a prerequisite for playing golf. But turning the body and swinging the golf club together create momentum. Therefore strength and control of the body are needed to control the clubhead: the legs for weight transference, the hands for gripping, the wrists and arms for hinging and leverage, and the midsection for turning.

Young people are inherently more physically fit than most seniors and certainly need less conditioning; but when you reach the age of say fifty or so, and still enjoy golf, you can extend your playing ability considerably through regular exercise.

Overall strength is improved by running, jogging, walking, or using weight-training devices. Specific exercises are designed to strengthen specific parts of the body, and a program for any golfer is best prescribed by a qualified person who is familiar with certain requirements for the basic golf swing; so, look for the many articles and books on the subject written by those who are well-qualified and search out well-qualified fitness centers where they can and will design specific exercises especially for your needs. It may be difficult to get started, but if you are not physically fit, physical fitness should become part of the challenge of playing well.

Flexibility

Just as all active persons in most sports are subject to injury, golfers also occasionally sustain injuries, particularly of the lower back. Consider what is involved in the golf swing, for instance: Throughout the golf swing the arms extend the clubhead outward, the clubhead is leveraged upward, the body is turning, the weight is shifting, and the upper body is turning against the lower body, all of which rely on muscles not only being strong but also being flexible.

According to the dictionary, *flexible* means "easily bent; not stiff; bending without breaking." Although muscles need to be strong to protect the vulnerable areas, they also need flexibility and resiliency in order not to be rigid or stiff, which causes tension—and tension in golf causes problems of its own.

Increasing flexibility helps relieve tension while increasing your range of motion and mobility. Specific drills are used that employ both stretching and isometric exercises for specific areas, thereby helping the body handle the strain of the swing to reduce the chance of injury.

Along with physical fitness, numerous flexibility drills may be found in books and magazines. Seniors in particular who want to play longer, better, and healthier should consider improving their physical well-being by strengthening their bodies with exercise and by using flexibility drills.

Health

Being healthy means being well and feeling good: being sound and wholesome and having strength and vigor. We know what promotes good health: practicing good nutrition, eating regular meals, drinking lots of water, getting plenty of rest and exercise, engaging in happy relationships, and having a good attitude. We also know of things that prevent good health, such as being unusually overweight.

Being overweight isn't always accurately measured by someone else's viewpoint of obesity. Although a stout player's primary problem may well be the one in front of him, many either heavily endowed or paunchy people maintain their weight at a certain level and, having learned to shift their weight and turn their shoulders, play golf exceedingly well. Being overweight is a problem, however, if your weight is too much in excess of what should be your normal weight. Even four or five more pounds around the middle—as is often the case—makes it more difficult to shift the weight and turn because increased weight causes loss of mobility.

Loss of mobility, especially in the legs and lower body, is a distinct disadvantage for any golfer because shifting the weight and turning the body coordinates with the hands and arms to swing the club and generate clubhead speed, and the legs initiate this action. It may seem no big deal if you become a little overweight; but then it also takes very little to lose some mobility.

Everyone has feelings and makes choices about how to live their lives, from choosing when and what they eat and drink to whether they even play golf. But when you eat and drink too much beyond normal consumption you are prone to gain too much weight. As well as adding calories, drinking too much has a narcotic effect that dulls your mind the next morning and tires your body later on; too much caffeine speeds up your backswing; and antianxiety pills make you too lethargic.

Whatever your goals, desires, or aspirations, if too much food, too much drink—or too much of anything, for that matter—causes problems, try some moderation. You just might improve your health, your disposition, and your life; and you definitely will improve your golf game. As an old English proverb says: "The joy of life is to live it." When it comes to living life and playing golf, dedicated golfers find that one enhances the other. They also find that with a little moderation they usually enhance them both.

PRACTICE

Practice is defined as "action done many times over for skill." While some people may naturally be more skillful than others, those less endowed quickly become more skillful with more practice. Regardless of natural ability, however, everything we do with any competency requires practice to develop skill.

Remember when you first learned how to catch and throw, swing a bat, ride a bike, roller-skate, or swim, for instance? Remember how you practiced and that the more you practiced, the more proficient you became? However, we can only practice what we learn through emulation, instruction, study, and experience.

Beyond emulation, as children we were instructed by parents, teachers, and our peers in the art of catching, throwing, swinging, and so on. Given the opportunity, and with further help and supervision, we then developed our proficiency with practice because "practicing" was play. So why not treat golf the same way? Because the game of golf is not just out the door and down the street for children at play, much less adults, and playing well takes both guidance and direction.

Although we grow up learning how to swing a club and hit a ball mostly through experience, unless instructed in basics the golf swing is not natural for most people until it becomes natural through understanding and practice. The result is that many players who just "took up" the game and may want to improve don't have a clue as to how or what to practice.

It is an absolute fact that productive practice and improvement requires knowledge about the golf swing. Knowing a little about a lot of things—or even a lot about just one thing—gives purpose and direction to practice; otherwise what's the point? Fun and exercise, perhaps. But hard-to-break bad habits are quickly ingrained in golf swings that have no purpose or direction. To overcome problems and improve in golf, not only do you need to know how and what but also when and where to practice as well as reasons why.

Practicing can be time-consuming, inconvenient, frustrating, and totally nonproductive; so serious practice is done by serious-minded golfers who practice what they've studied and what they've learned through instruction and experience. They accept the challenge of playing better and are dedicated to improvement. As essayist Bernard Darwin explained it, "It is this constant and undying hope for improvement that makes golf so exquisitely worth the playing."

Aside from being an "undying hope for improvement," the obvious reason for practice is to develop, correct, or change your golf swing in order to hit the ball farther and straighter, make the difficult golf shots, and play with pride and self-esteem. But practicing is not just relegated to honing your skills on a driving range because your short game accounts for over half the shots you play.

With chipping estimated as thirteen percent and putting as forty-three percent of the game, once your swing is halfway reliable your short game needs as much, if not more, time for practice in order to start pitching with precision, chipping closer, and putting more accurately.

Whatever or wherever you practice, fringe benefits are that you strengthen your hands, improve coordination, develop muscle memory, develop "feel" for making golf shots, and develop your confidence and concentration (Illustration 3.6). The more you practice off the course, the more you will enjoy playing; the flip side is that playing the course is where you find the weakest part of your game and practicing is where you fix or improve it. Aside from that, you practice your golf swing to improve in golf so you can enjoy playing the game. And the more you meet the challenge, of course, the more you enjoy playing.

What you practice should depend on two things: (1) your level of expertise and (2) what you find to be the weakest part of your game. Anyone just starting golf needs to practice the grip and set-up, as well as basic movements, while experienced golfers should still check out the basics from time to time, but practice swing techniques that combine accuracy and consistency. All players should always practice chipping and putting to further develop "touch and feel" as a means of maintaining confidence.

3.6 Practicing concentration, confidence, and "touch and feel."

Once you understand requirements for the basic golf swing, as well as understanding the importance of practice, you also need to practice pre-swing procedure (Illustration 3.7). Vastly underrated in golf instruction, this pre-swing routine is the very foundation for a sound, repeating golf swing. Through repetition you develop balance and coordination and get a running start on continuity and accuracy throughout the rest of your swing.

Practicing depends more on quality than on quantity; so, rather than just quickly dispersing golf balls willy-nilly on a driving range, the first thing

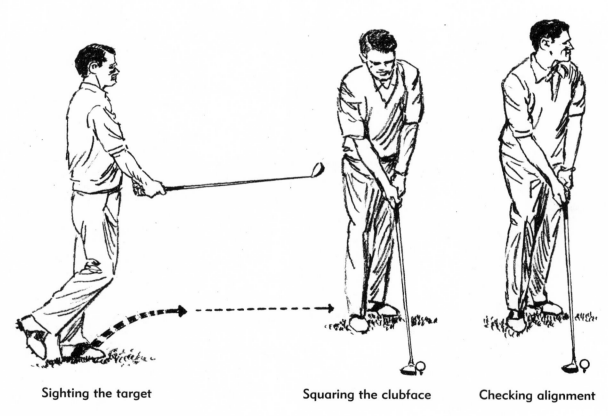

Sighting the target   Squaring the clubface   Checking alignment

3.7 Pre-swing procedure provides the "ready, set, go!"

to practice is patience. It takes patience to practice intelligently. It also takes intelligence to practice patience.

Having guidelines for practice helps develop a procedure for improvement not provided for by just hitting balls at random. Allow yourself plenty of time for practice, don't try to practice everything at once, and always have a goal in mind and a target in sight. To attain that goal also practice the following procedures:

1. Stretch your muscles with a flexibility drill or two, then start your practice with warm-up practice swings.

Squaring positions The pre-swing waggle Ready to go

2. Always hit toward a target and occasionally use your golf clubs to check your alignment (Illustration 3.8). Check to see that your clubface is square to the target (A); your feet are square to the clubface (B); your knees, hips, and shoulders are square to your feet and clubface (C); then visualize your swing path and waggle the clubhead back and forth a bit on the target line (D). Having checked your alignment, you may want to remove the foot alignment club but leave the other club during practice so you may continue to check the angle of your clubface and your clubhead path.

3. Use a tee in practice if it helps with confidence. Hitting better golf shots helps you build more confidence.

4. To help with tempo and improve your timing, start by hitting short irons somewhat short of their normal distance, then develop a feel for distance by alternating both short and longer shots.

Ideally, practicing should be done whenever you have the time. At no time, however, is it more important than when you are taking lessons. Just before playing, however, practicing should be relegated to just loosening up your muscles with good tempo and timing.

Although opportunities for self-improvement in golf are endless, especially through practice, one thing still eludes most players: being knowledgeable enough about problems that do occur within your own golf swing in order to be able to overcome them. Hence the value of understanding the golf swing itself.

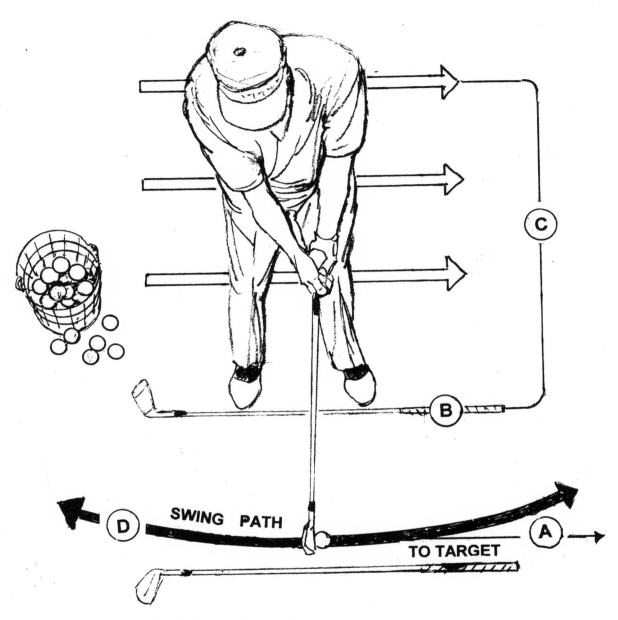

3.8 . . . and occasionally check your alignment!

CHAPTER FOUR

Ability
The Power to Perform or Accomplish

Certainly those with inherently good coordination in golf—often construed as "natural ability"—will possibly start earlier, play more, and probably even score better than others. Since neither gender, shape, size, nor age denote one's ability, however, those with less "natural" ability need never fare less well in their enjoyment of the game because both coordination and ability can increasingly become more natural (Illustration 4.1).

The "power to perform or accomplish" in golf is first cultivated by desire and motivation, of course, followed by knowledge, practice, and persistence. For instance: (1) Desire generally starts with observation, association, and encouragement from others who already play golf.

THIN   SHORT   TALL

SENIOR   JUNIOR   STOUT

4.1 Neither gender, shape, size, nor age denote one's ability.

(2) Motivation is an incentive to play better coupled with a desire for self-improvement. (3) Knowledge is "all that is known or can be learned"—which should always include taking lessons in golf because knowledge is not sufficiently gained by just playing. (4) Practice results from having acquired knowledge coupled with a strong motivation to improve performance. (5) And, finally, persistence in spite of everything is a strong determination to play the game to the best of one's ability.

Although a desire to play golf may originate at any age, very rarely are desire and ability packaged together and labeled "natural." *Au contraire.* In 1981 Sam Snead, famed for his natural golf swing and a paragon in the golfing world, wrote, "I'd like to have a quarter for every shot I hooked with my natural grip before I developed the unnatural grip that let me hit them straighter." And Ben Hogan acknowledged that there is absolutely "nothing natural" about the golf swing.

The difference between golf professionals and average players is certainly ability, of course. But golf is big-time business with professionals who are highly motivated and work full-time at their chosen field of endeavor, as you do. Consider the fact, though, that if professionals worked far less and you worked harder at golf, the gap between your abilities would narrow. The professional's level of performance might decrease, having already maximized ability, but yours would increase because you improved your ability through knowledge, practice, and persistence.

The primary reason so many players play poorly is not due to lack of ability but to the way they took up the game. Rather than learning basics and swing mechanics by taking lessons, men often take up golf by just swinging fast and hitting hard with the single objective of hitting the ball as far as possible. On the other hand, women are prone to swing easier, trying just to hit it. Without guidance and direction, however, many of these would-be golfers develop bad swings and play poorly, become intimidated and frustrated, lose interest in the game, and subsequently lose the opportunity to develop their own ability.

Although the golf swing itself stems from natural movements of both swinging and hitting, and there are many golfers who play with "natural talent" due to good coordination, the golf swing itself is not natural. We do nothing naturally where the body turns rotationally as the arms swing upward with the hands gripped together. The more proficient you become, however, the more natural these movements become.

Physical ability is not a prerequisite for learning to play golf but physical fitness is always a factor in attaining proficiency in any athletic endeavor. Being considerably overweight is a problem, for instance, because it inhibits turning of the upper body while preventing mobility of the legs and lower body. And lack of exercise prevents developing muscles that promote flexibility, extension, and strength, all of which are needed for the golf swing.

As whimsically noted by a renowned British golf writer, Peter Dobereiner, "Golf itself is not exactly an athletic activity or exercise that results in either muscle toning or loss of weight as a result of physical exhaustion. Golf is not energetic enough for a muscular tonic. For sweating off surplus poundage," he wrote, "you would be better off with a furious game of dominoes." Although ostensibly correct perhaps, when sufficiently motivated much can be done with diet and conditioning to improve one's physical ability.

ABILITY

Anyone can learn to play golf. But what makes golf so complex and frustrating for those who want to play well or play better generally is not lack of ability but lack of knowledge about the basic golf swing as well as lack of practice and dedication. You develop your ability, though, through correct application of swing mechanics that improve your physical skills through practice.

•

CHAPTER FIVE

Balance and Coordination

Nothing can be regarded as unimportant in the golf swing because one thing builds on another in a chain reaction. Along with alignment, body positions are of utmost importance because they promote correct movements. In turn, movements interact with each other for balance and coordination.

Certainly everyone has balance and coordination in common to some degree, whether golfers or not, but proficient golfers are prone to further develop these assets because balance and coordination are the essence of a good golf swing.

Balance and coordination result from all positions and movements that combine the actions of both swinging and hitting around a steady head position. Although golfers frequently are advised to "swing easy and hit hard," neither can be well negotiated without these basics.

BALANCE

Balance throughout the swing begins with pre-established positions that promote a balanced setup. Because of this, requirements for the swing are explicit about establishing positions that provide good posture and weight distribution. Also, the width of your stance and position of your feet are all-important in the setup because balance at address is the keystone for good footwork.

Maintaining balance and using good footwork is a solution to many swing problems, but footwork in itself is not controlled by conscious thought; rather, footwork is the result of feet reacting naturally to pre-established positions as they respond to other swing movements. For instance, to sense the feeling of your feet in a balanced swinging movement, separate your feet, keep your arms at your side, completely turn your shoulders right and left, and just let your feet and arms respond (Illustration 5.1; A). Notice how your weight shifts right, then left, and your heels pull up and inward as you maintain balance? Now use this same footwork and balance to turn your body and swing your arms around (B). These are naturally coordinated movements that are also used in golf (C).

Both balance and coordination in golf originate from lower-body action where good footwork is the mainstay: the very foundation for your golf swing. Coordinating lower-body with upper-body action enables the counterpart of good footwork, namely good hand action, to help release the clubhead through the hitting zone. To negotiate this, however, you must do

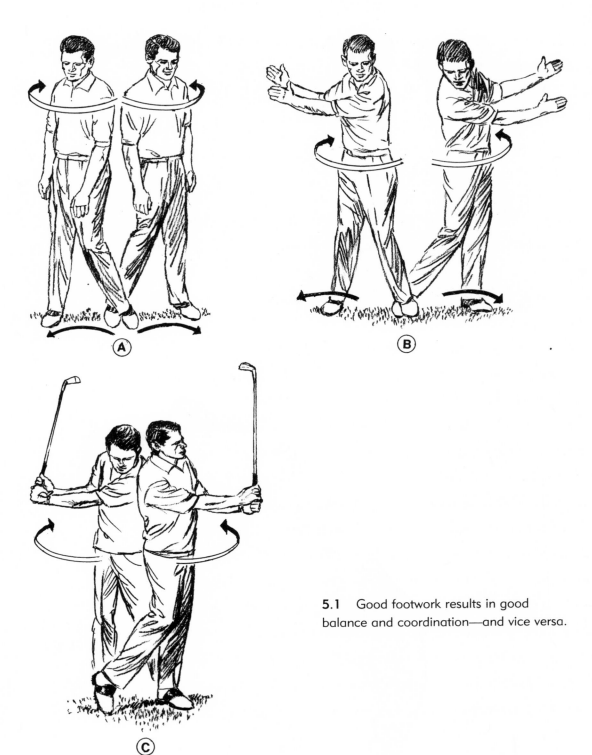

5.1 Good footwork results in good balance and coordination—and vice versa.

everything possible—both physically and mentally—to help the downswing start with the *lower* body moving first from the top of the swing. This requires holding the head fairly steady while turning the body and swinging at a pace that allows positions time to coordinate with each other.

COORDINATION

Coordination is the harmonious adjustment, or working together, of all parts of the body, most of which is natural in golf but some of which is not. Learning about the "mechanics" of the golf swing helps one learn what is natural, as well as learning how to make more natural the movements that are not.

It helps to understand, therefore, that most components of the golf swing originate from certain body movements that already coordinate—movements such as shifting your weight and swinging your arms while walking or running, for instance. These same natural movements also coordinate the hands with the feet, the arms with the legs, and the hips with the shoulders, and so on.

Although coordination and balance throughout your swing result from things that do occur naturally, such as good footwork and good hand action, you still need to know what does *not* occur naturally in order to avoid unnecessary problems. For example, unlike the more naturally coordinated movements of a baseball swing, where the body and the arms all turn rotationally, the golf swing requires the body to turn rotationally while the arms swing upright together. It seems easier and far more natural, therefore, to move all the parts in the same direction, to swing "flat"—or *around*—with a baseball bat, for instance, than to swing more *upright* with a golf club.

Therefore, parts of the body that coordinate naturally outside of golf often need encouragement to work together in golf.

Because the golf swing feels unnatural with its rotational pivot and upright swing, the tendency is to make serious swing errors such as swinging flat, "picking up the clubhead," "hitting from the top" with the arms and hands, and "falling away from the ball" in a "reverse weight shift." Since that's what the body would rather do naturally, it is important to understand, apply, and practice things that feel unnatural until they become more natural.

All positions and movements from the start of the swing are programmed to help the weight shift back then shift forward from the top of the swing. So, it all comes down to this: With knowledge and practice, *the downswing starts with the lower body moving first in order to pull the hands, arms, and clubhead down from the top.* Otherwise, either one of two destructive problems may occur: (1) Either the upper body starts the downswing *with* the hands and arms, thereby either "hitting from the top" with the hands or else "coming over the top" with the right shoulder; or (2) when players understand its importance, they often try to *start* the downswing with their hands or arms without completing their backswing. This shorter backswing then prevents the shoulders from turning against the hips to create a necessary "torque-then-release" of the lower body that pulls the clubhead down.

Although many positions and movements in golf are natural, and those that are not become so with understanding, dedication, and practice, there also are four not-so-natural swing *actions* that occur to help blend the swing together: extension, the weight shift, swinging upright, and completing the shoulder turn. Although all of these are compatible and each enhances the other, promoting one without the others will not enhance the golf swing. You need to understand and apply them all to avoid problems.

Extension or Extensor Action

Extension in golf is a reaching out or stretching of the arms throughout the golf swing (Illustration 5.2): the left arm through the backswing (A) and the right arm through impact (B). Although the right arm folds into the backswing and the left arm folds into the follow-through, extension of one

5.2 Extensor action means extension.

arm still stretches and strengthens the other—but only to the extent that the other allows a structured, extensor action, or stretching of the muscles.

Extensor action is effective throughout the swing, but it is best understood as the unfolding and straightening of the right arm through impact that stretches and strengthens the left arm.

Combined with good tempo, extension of the left arm through the *backswing* helps keep the left arm firm and strong, initiates a big swing arc, and helps create clubhead speed. Also, as your firm left arm extends and stretches with the folding of your right arm, notice how your left wrist strengthens and straightens to return this power in concert with extension of the right arm through impact.

Bobby Jones once wrote, "The greater the extension or stretching, the greater the force of the return. In the golf swing, every inch added to the backward windup, up to the limit at which the balance of the body can be easily maintained, represents additional stored energy available to increase the power of the downswing."

Although it appears that a big extension into the backswing would pull the body laterally into swaying rather than turning, swaying is prevented by every position at address that promotes good balance and coordination: namely, strong legs, good footwork, the weight shift, and definitely the shoulder turn.

Weight Shift

Nothing improves a bad golf swing more than a correct weight shift, and nothing makes a good swing worse than shifting the weight in a manner contradictory to a natural swinging movement.

In the golf swing, as in any sporting event or athletic endeavor where balance and coordination underwrite success or failure, weight must move in the same direction as motion. In golf, in other words, the weight must shift in unison with the swinging movement—to the right as the club moves away from the ball and to the left as the club pulls downward and moves on into the follow-through. Turning and weight shift therefore complement each other. Turning the body helps shift the weight to the right; shifting the weight helps turn the shoulders; and completing the shoulder turn also turns the hips. When keeping the head steady as well, this creates torque, whereupon reflex action then helps start the downswing with the *lower* body, back first. They all go hand-in-hand. The weight shifting forward then pulls the hands, arms, and clubhead down and through the hitting zone with power and accuracy: hence the importance of the weight shift.

Shifting the weight in golf is similar to walking (Illustration 5.3). The difference, however, is that, unlike walking, where moving parts all move forward in the same direction (A), in golf the feet "walk" sideways as the body turns rotationally (B and C). Now if the body moved sideways also, there would be no problem with this; but then that naturally comfortable, lateral movement also known as "swaying" occurs, which is why we have *that* problem. Swaying laterally rather than turning is deadly in the golf swing; but forewarned is forearmed, as they say, which should help you avoid the problem.

Just as you can prevent swaying when you know and understand the problem, you can also prevent a reverse weight shift, where the weight incorrectly shifts to the left through the backswing and to the right on the downswing or forward swing, by practicing prevention.

5.3 When you turn your body and swing your arms, the weight shift is just like walking.

Although shifting the weight incorrectly creates its own swing problems, momentum through the backswing adds a certain amount of stress to left arm firmness, especially if you are swinging too fast. So, a major problem to avoid at the top of the swing as the downswing starts is a weakening or bending of the firm left arm. Here's why: As the weight changes direction during the transition of the backswing to the downswing, the "whiplash" effect may force

61

the left arm to bend (Illustration 5.4). Few things are more destructive than losing left arm firmness throughout the backswing and downswing, however, because it immediately loses the leverage being created by the shoulders against the hips for power and distance.

Hundreds of articles of instruction have been written about how to shift the weight, as well as where weight should or shouldn't be from address to follow-through. Three things of importance to remember are: (1) the body must turn; (2) the weight must shift away from the ball through the backswing and toward the ball into the forward swing; and (3) balance must be maintained. It takes knowledge of the movement as well as patience and practice. Remember, though, that basic positions and swing movements required by the golf swing really will coordinate to make your golf swing work.

As Bobby Jones once wrote, "The downswing develops a very high speed by the time it reaches the ball, but the acceleration should be gradual in order to attain control and preserve balance. It helps a lot to realize that there is plenty of time. A backswing of ample length and a leisurely start downward will avoid a peck of trouble."

Completing the Shoulder Turn

The length of the backswing, if thought of at all, probably is thought of only as how far back the

5.4 How to lose coordination.

clubhead goes. Although a parallel shaft at the top of the swing is generally considered "normal," exactly how far the clubhead travels is relatively unimportant compared with whether control of the clubhead is being maintained at the top of the swing. The rest of the swing depends on this control as determined by the strength and flexibility of the player; a firm left arm and left hand grip; tempo and timing; the weight shift; and, of course, the shoulder turn.

Every golfer needs to complete a fairly "level" shoulder turn and pivot within their own capability (Illustration 5.5; A), rather than letting the left knee and shoulder dip downward (B). Completing the shoulder turn then helps return the shoulders to square through impact (C) as a residual result of good coordination between the upper and lower body as opposed to the right shoulder "coming over the top" (D).

Here's how it works: First of all, the arms are positioned together at address with a firm left arm but with a relaxed right arm slightly lower than the left (Illustration 5.6; A). Once positioned together, the arms then swing together simply by *keeping* them together throughout the swing into a completion of the follow-through (B). Meanwhile, the hands and clubface are positioned "square" at address (Illustration 5.7; A), so just keeping the arms together and pushing the clubhead away into a "toe-up" position (B) starts the right elbow pointing downward as the right arm folds. In turn, this starts the shoulder turn, which turns the hips (C). Automatically then, as shown again in Illustration 5.7 (B), the arms, hands, and clubhead move into and through a position in the backswing where the toe of the clubhead points straight up, the thumbs are on top, the left wrist is straight, and the shaft of the club is parallel to the line of the feet.

5.5 Controlling the clubhead.

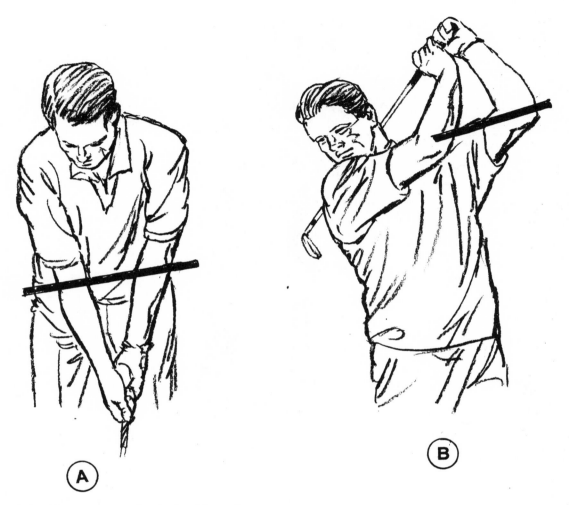

5.6 Your arms put the "swing" in golf . . .

Keeping the arms together and keeping the left wrist straight through the wrist break while completing the shoulder turn not only moves the clubhead on the right swing path, but a firm left arm and folding right arm helps wedge the clubhead upward. Along with extension, this wedging upward action of the arms and elbows not only promotes turning, rather than moving laterally, but also results in a naturally correct wrist break.

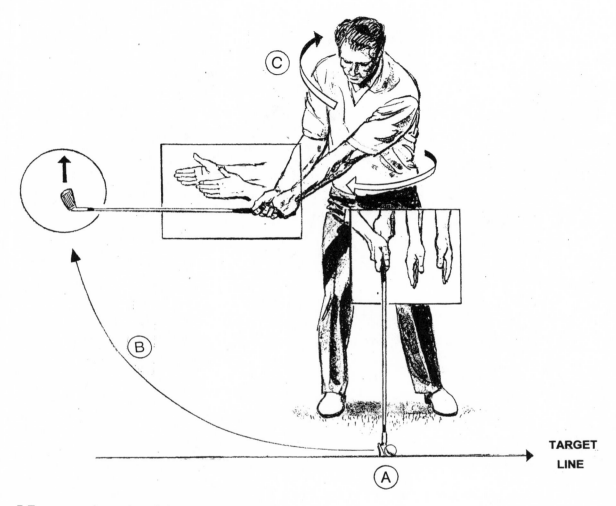

5.7 . . . and your hands keep it all together.

Your shoulder turn can either be your best asset or your worst liability in golf. Whereas correctly completing the shoulder turn increases power and accuracy, a large percentage of players are so anxious to hit the ball with only their hands that they seldom, if ever, negotiate a full shoulder turn. Of course, this only negates the advantages by promoting swinging flat rather than swinging upright.

Swinging Upright

Swinging flat instead of upright is a chronic problem in golf that prevents coordination needed to return the clubface square. The problem results from starting the swing by rolling the hands horizontally, or "roundhouse" style, into the backswing. The key to *not* swinging flat, therefore, is learning more about hand action.

Repeated application of all positions and movements that promote a correct wrist break and completed shoulder turn helps promote good hand action by wedging the hands, arms, and clubhead upward. Swinging upright then positions the hands to pull straight downward from the top of the swing (Illustration 5.8; A). However, as the shoulders turn and the movement is away from the ball, there often is a tendency to "roll" the hands and wrists back to "lay" the club back flat (B). Swinging flat, however, prevents the hands from pulling downward from the top of the swing to hit squarely through the hitting zone (C) by positioning them to pull forward (D).

From the same clubhead "toe-up" position as previously shown in Illustration 5.7 (B), though, keeping the left wrist straight and continuing to cock the hands straight upward will correctly complete the backswing.

Swinging upright results in overall accuracy as the hands return to hit squarely through the hitting zone into a high, completed follow-through (see Illustration 5.8, part C) while swinging flat results in varied and distinctively creative golf shots resulting from a "roundhouse" follow-through (see Illustration 5.8, part D).

Difficulty swinging upright generally stems from using the hands to swing the clubhead rather than from using the weight shift and shoulder turn. But swinging upright has an additional guideline to help you keep your swing on track: Simply guide your hands upward to above your right

5.8 Up and down—not 'round and 'round.

shoulder on the backswing and up above your left shoulder in the follow-through, as in Illustration 5.8, parts A and C.

Unless the hands are positioned at the top of the swing to be pulled straight downward, the swing is too flat. And how can you tell in your own golf swing? At impact the shoulders return to open rather than square, the clubhead returns from outside-in as a result of "coming over the top," and you've probably lost your golf ball. It doesn't have to happen, however, if you practice basics as prescribed for the basic golf swing.

Recognizing and Dealing with Problems

The magnitude of problems encountered in golf is staggering, so much so that many hundreds of books and articles, as well as helpful pointers, quick tips, instant fixes, "keys," and so on, have been written on how to overcome them. However, in spite of all the help and all we learn and understand, because of our physical inability to attain perfection and our mental inability to withstand the pressure, problems will always occur in golf.

Obviously the object of golf is to play the course in as few strokes as possible; but something always seems to go wrong somewhere, to some degree, to increase the score. Because of the multitude of "things" that make up the swing, however, it takes very little to make small problems even worse in golf.

Simply defined, problems are "things that cause difficulty." So, problems in golf may refer to anything: positions or movements, difficulty of the golf course itself, poor concentration, other players' poor behavior, your own emotional outbursts, down to and including inclement weather and bad luck. However, although a moot subject, perhaps, hooking, slicing, pulling, pushing, topping, shanking, skying, skulling, smothering, toeing, whiffing, or hitting behind the ball (known as sclaffing), for instance, are not problems in themselves *because all of these are only game-wrecking results of the underlying problem of a poor golf swing.*

Although individually detailed correction for such poor results as these may be found in many well-written golf books, problems with either positions or movements that cause these poor results are minimized or even eliminated by fine-tuning your mental awareness and expanding your knowledge to improve your golf swing. Recognizing and dealing with problems is only one more facet in meeting the challenge of playing well.

Problems commonly start at address with something quite minor such as being a little bit off with alignment, reaching too far with the weight on the toes, positioning the ball a little too far back or forward, positioning the right hand "under" with the palm facing skyward, and so on. Problems then multiply when the clubhead starts a little too much either "inside" or "outside," the backswing starts a little too fast, the hands get a little too active, the body moves a little bit laterally, and so on and so forth.

Knowledge that improves both mental awareness and ability is still one's front-line defense against the never-ending complexity of the game itself. A little bit of knowledge helps us recognize and overcome such things as emotional upsets or attitude flaws and a lot of knowledge helps us recognize and deal with any number of swing defects and poor results.

Many suggestions throughout this book focus on the importance of not only you and your golf game, but also on things such as taking lessons; upgrading equipment; employing the use of books, magazines, and visual aids; course management; physical fitness; practice; and so on. One thing still remains, however, that eludes most players: being able to recognize problems when they do occur and being able to correct them.

Remember the sage advice, "Don't fix it if it ain't broke?" Well, you can't fix it if you don't *know* it's "broke" and neither can you fix it if you don't know *what's* "broke." In other words, if you start slicing and you know the origin of slicing can be either an incorrect grip or stance at address that caused an incorrect golf swing, you then can deduce what may be wrong in your own golf swing because you know what is right. In turn, knowing what is right enables you to fix the problem. Professionally this is known as "error detection and correction."

Being able to help yourself with your own golf swing is a major satisfaction in golf and certainly part of the challenge. Ben Hogan once emphasized that point when he said, "The novice player should be happy every day because every day he should find something new to improve." But just as a doctor needs to be a good analyst to help a patient, and a teaching professional a good analyst to help a student, you must be a good analyst to help yourself.

Requirements for being a good analyst are twofold: First, you need to recognize when your swing is "broke" so you know *when* to fix it; this includes knowing and understanding yourself as well as recognizing poor results. Second, so that you know *how* to fix it, you need to know and understand requirements for the basic swing to know what is correct or incorrect in your own swing.

It may seem like a new way of thinking or a new method to follow, but the closer you come to what is correct, both at address and through the swing, and the more you understand and cope with your own deficiencies, the more you eliminate the problems that cause the poor results. And the more you eliminate, of course, the more worthwhile the effort.

As Jack Nicklaus noted in his book *Golf My Way,* "Any method, old or new, will fail if, first, it is not founded on sound fundamentals and, second, if the golfer trying to master it will not force or train or cajole himself into mastering those fundamentals before he attends to the frills." But be encouraged. The more knowledgeable you become and the more you work toward improvement, thereby meeting the challenge, the more proficient you become. With that in mind, I wrote *How to Master a Great Golf Swing* especially for the purpose of helping you be able to help yourself.

PART III

The Mental Aspect of Golf

CHAPTER SEVEN

Attitude

A Learned Predisposition to Respond to People, Objects, or Institutions in a Positive or Negative Way

There is a saying, "If you want to know a person well, play golf with them." Although this is true of others, it is particularly true when that person is yourself. No matter what the competition, the challenge will always be to win the one that reigns within yourself that influences power, supremacy, and control. So how do you win this inner game of golf? You start by learning how not to beat yourself with your own negative attitude.

Your attitude and the results of your golf game go hand-in-hand. One promotes the other. Simply stated, a negative attitude promotes poor performance and poor results while a positive attitude promotes good performance and good results. Consider this: You arrive at the golf course with an upbeat, positive attitude with high hopes for a great golf game. If you play badly, though, it becomes increasingly difficult to maintain a positive attitude, which then adversely affects your performance.

Whatever the situation, a change in attitude from positive to negative quickly manifests itself in any number of ways: anger, frustration, impatience, intolerance, despair, self-pity, and so on—any or all of which only compound problems. However, getting angry, frustrated, impatient, or whatever, not only ruins concentration and timing but causes pressure and performance anxieties that result in tension and stress.

Your whole golf game is affected by adverse changes in your attitude. But you also form attitudes and present yourself to others by how you respond to everyone and everything you encounter in golf.

Problems in golf that affect one's feelings and attitude seem so insurmountable at times that you may wonder how others overcome them to avoid negativism. Well, others don't always surmount them, of course, but there is a way to overcome problems if they aren't too complex. It's just an application of awareness.

Bringing clearly into focus whatever may prevent you from attaining your potential helps you maintain control of yourself and your golf game. If the problem is frustration, fix your golf swing; if the problem is other golfers, practice tolerance; if it's slow play, practice patience. Whatever the problem may be, recognizing and dealing with it will quickly upgrade your attitude and prevent its sudden, quick-change-artistry on the golf course.

Because others form conclusions based only on what they see, it appears to them that one loses in golf because of physical manifestations of a poor golf game. They only see the physical result of missed tee shots, topped fairway woods, skulled chip shots, and the like, whereas we tend to view these same results of our own golf swing as mental. Although we know intellectually that poor swing mechanics cause most poor shots, rather than blaming our golf swing we tend to blame ourselves. We call ourselves a "really dumb jerk" or whatever else may be expedient. But these thoughts create negative feelings. And, because you are what you perceive yourself to be, you see yourself as such, the result of which is dejection and frustration (Illustration 7.1). The problems are still physical, though, and they become even more pronounced throughout a round of golf when we succumb to negative thinking. Although negative thinking is destructive, it can be eradicated because negativism is self-taught.

We tend to measure ourselves by our accomplishments in golf; but golf is what you do, not what you are. When you call yourself a "really dumb jerk" you demean yourself and lower your self-esteem. When you tell yourself, "I'm no good because I made a lousy golf shot," you are dwelling on what might have been or could have been while crowding out more positive thoughts about the next golf shot.

POSITIVE THINKING

Positive thinking has forever been touted in the world of psychology as "a highly effective approach to important life issues." In golf as well as in life, therefore, the essence of positive thinking is to focus on where you want to go and what you want to do rather than on where you don't want to go and

7.1 You are what you see and feel yourself to be.

what you don't want to do. "I can do it!" is a powerful medium that facilitates positive thinking; however, the foundation for positive thinking in golf is having a reliable golf swing that gives you confidence and control.

Accepting Yourself and Your Abilities

You are who you think you are in life, but you also have the power to be who you want to be. This holds true in golf as well. But to be who you want to be, you need to have a positive attitude that directs your mind toward things that are realistic so you can enhance your ability to accomplish them.

The first step is to seek professional or qualified help in developing your natural talents and golfing abilities; the second is to try hard, but to accept yourself and your abilities; and the third step is to avoid the ultimate trap of settling only for perfection. Work within a positive framework and measure yourself by how many good shots you make rather than by poor ones.

Playing within Yourself

Learning to play within yourself results from accepting yourself and your abilities. By doing so you overcome the pitfall of performance anxiety. There's nothing wrong with being the shortest hitter off the tee—unless your ego sees it as a flaw in performance and tells your brain you're weak and dumb. No one in your foursome sees it that way. And neither should you try to hit beyond your proven range or get more distance with too short a club.

Surprisingly, perhaps—but a lesson for your ego—no one is as interested in your game as you are, no matter what. But then neither are you as interested in theirs. Not that we all are that disinterested or non-supportive. But golf is a very selfish game in that you are playing against yourself, and golfers who effectively win that game are absorbed with their own performance and their own golf game. A case in point, for instance: Following a round of golf, how many times have you experienced someone's difficulty (perhaps yours?) recalling the name of the fourth person with whom they played that day? Possibly that lapse of memory is indicative of what golfers think about.

Maximizing Your Performance

Nothing will improve your attitude more quickly than improving your golf swing, whereupon performance improves two ways: (1) your mind is free to focus on making golf shots; and (2) the more you successfully make your golf shots, the more your confidence improves.

Learn to accept things as they are and maintain a positive attitude. There always will be seemingly unfair golf holes and unfair occurrences to be overcome such as tough rough, bad lies, bad bounces, and so on. But you are not the only one who has to deal with all these things; they are the same things all players have to be concerned with at whatever level of golf they play. It helps to remember this. That's golf. That's the way it is. Meet the challenge of adversity by not preoccupying your mind with all the bad luck you have.

Take advantage of your practice time. The practice range is where you practice everything, where mistakes should be made so they can be corrected, and where you learn to control your emotions. With less pressure to succeed or perform and more emphasis on overall improvement, the practice range is also a good place to practice patience and self control, for instance, and to improve both concentration and confidence.

What you learn in practice you apply on the golf course. You learn to play at a calmer pace that allows you to relax somewhat both physically and mentally. You find yourself better able to focus on applying your physical skills. The ability to relax and play each hole, one shot at a time, whatever happens, is a great asset.

Improving Your Disposition

Knowing yourself as a person is one thing, but knowing yourself as a golfer is a real eye-opener, leaving you to wonder at times just where that other person with a surprisingly bizarre disposition came from. Also, your behavior on the golf course exposes you to others, showing others how you think and feel. A nice disposition makes golf enjoyable for everyone so it behooves you as a person to be a pleasant golfer with a pleasant disposition.

Our disposition is a compilation of our many beliefs and attitudes as well as personality traits that characterize each of us as individuals. Disposition is influenced by our natural or usual way of thinking about things, and affects how we act toward others: cheerful, argumentative, easy-going, or hard to get along with—which is probably why we all are so different. We naturally and predictably think about and view things differently.

Strongly influenced by feelings and emotions in golf, your disposition and temperament—or how you feel at the moment—helps determine your ability to stay focused and concentrate: two essential ingredients that help you stay on-track. It helps considerably, therefore, not to have an explosive nature as you encounter changes in your circumstances.

Being able to keep your wits about you after driving into a fairway bunker enables you to meet the challenge of getting out of the bunker by helping you immediately start concentrating on your next golf shot (Illustration 7.2; A). On the other hand, being predisposed to anger or dejection over hitting into a fairway bunker prevents you from concentrating on your next shot because your mind still dwells on the tee shot (B). A noticeable difference in a person's disposition can readily be detected in a golfer's posture and countenance. Cultivating qualities such as patience, flexibility, and composure therefore helps us maintain a disposition and posture that help us deal with adversity in golf.

7.2 Composure overcomes adversity.

Patience is the ability to maintain calm endurance under any circumstance without complaining or losing self-control. Certainly nowhere is this a more valuable asset than in golf, where you constantly meet the challenge of adversity, where everyone (except your own foursome, of course) plays too fast or too slow and your ball rolls into trouble instead of out all day.

Nothing except your own frustration, perhaps, tests your disposition more quickly than continually being held up by players in front of you or else being hit into by inconsiderate players behind you. But losing patience over something so uncontrollable as what other players do only diminishes your own level of play. It seems helpful instead to try to speed up or slow down your own group's level of play to keep a lock on patience and composure. Certainly both are needed for playing and making golf shots.

Just as you need to change your thinking every time you play a golf shot, you have to be flexible with other players who may act and think differently from you. A little patience exercised at precisely the right moment may be just what your scorecard needs. Practicing patience when your disposition leans toward *im*patience can be just as important as practicing your golf swing.

Flexibility is the ability to adapt to a situation or circumstance. Since this relates to almost everything in golf, including another's bad behavior, to prevent becoming "one of those" it pays to practice being completely flexible.

Being flexible in your thinking and accepting adversity enables you to accept as a challenge not only imperfection in others but also your own substandard golf shots and bad lies. It enables you to maintain composure while effectively planning to either play the ball from where it lies or else take the penalty. You can control your golf game only so long as you control yourself—and you are not in control if you let another player, a bad shot, or an occasional bad lie wreck your whole golf game because you couldn't adapt to a situation.

Composure is calmness and self-control regulated by feelings and emotions. From the frustration of slow play to the thrill of getting a hole-in-one, composure, as opposed to constant mood swings, is an important asset in golf. It keeps you focused on the moment that entails concentrating on the next golf shot as well as on playing the rest of the game to the best of your ability.

Pressure comes from inside yourself as well as from outside sources according to how you let things affect your thinking or influence your level of play; so, be aware that you may either win or lose the game as a result of how you mentally adapt to meet the challenges. Then finally, to enjoy the game more while meeting those challenges, try applying the old adage: "Hope for the best, prepare for the worst, and take whatever comes with a smile."

CHAPTER EIGHT

Personality
Unique and Enduring Behavior Patterns

Our disposition on the golf course is how our personality is expressed, and our personality is how we are judged by others. While we observe and learn about others—and they about us—we also learn more about our own disposition and about ourselves.

Others continually influence our thinking and actions as we grow and develop. Not only do our family, friends, teachers, and coworkers influence us, we also are influenced by our physical and cultural environment. The result is that we eventually develop feelings and emotions and a certain way of responding until even our character is influenced by how others react to us.

As we encounter and adjust to all of life's experiences, we become who and what we are, with a distinctive personality. In golf, therefore, it helps to understand how personality traits in general influence one's ability to perform.

Personality traits are "relatively permanent and enduring qualities that a person shows in most situations." Mixtures of these traits help make us different from each other as well as different in our many endeavors such as golf. As long as these characteristics are most typical of your behavior, they also are considered fairly stable traits of your personality.

In the field of psychology, studies describe many personality traits that refer to personal characteristics. As a point of interest, some have been listed as follows:

EXAMPLES OF PERSONALITY TRAITS

Addictive	Daring	Obedient
Aggressive	Dishonest	Organized
Ambitious	Emotional	Paranoid
Bold	Flexible	Passionate
Cautious	Friendly	Polite
Charming	Generous	Sadistic
Cheerful	Genial	Selfish
Clever	Humble	Sensitive
Clumsy	Impetuous	Shy
Compulsive	Jealous	Sociable
Confident	Kind	Stoic
Controlling	Loyal	Thoughtful
Creative	Meticulous	Wayward
Crude	Nervous	

Behavior refers to "actions usually measured by commonly accepted standards." For example, although we often try to disguise our true selves at times to create a good impression, we inadvertently expose ourselves to others by what we say and how we act. Unless we truly are what we present ourselves to be and our personality traits are strong enough to withstand stress and tension, traits we normally display in everyday situations, such as courtesy and patience, may suddenly translate into discourtesy and impatience on the golf course. Instantly, then, these intermix with other traits or feelings such as anger or frustration. In other words, an otherwise very nice golfer may chunk the ball off the tee into the water, suddenly utter atrocious obscenities, then throw the club in too.

Regardless of the fact that we can—and do—control our feelings or emotions under normal circumstances, few of us (if any) can control all of our emotions on the golf course. This is why your golf swing is best transformed into subconscious behavior, so you can better deal emotionally with disruptive situations while your swing stays intact. As Bobby Jones wrote in 1929, "The golf swing is a most complicated combination of muscular actions, too complex to be controlled by objective conscious mental effort."

When we cannot consciously control our golf swing and our personality is such that we cannot control our emotions, our whole golf game is vulnerable to disruption—and often total destruction—by anger, fear, frustration, and so on. Any of these can suddenly turn us either cowardly or ballistic on the golf course because our image of ourselves as in control of our mind and muscles has been shattered. Or perhaps we think we deserve to play better because we try so hard. Neither viewpoint is realistic, however, unless or until we earn it, in this case by learning more about how to control ourselves and our behavior.

Behavior patterns of touring professionals generally differ considerably from those of average players. Not because they were born with composure and disciplined behavior that only touring professionals possess. Certainly not. Rather, they've channeled years of mental energy into dealing with personal deficiencies, as well as into controlling their emotions, in order to improve their performance. You can do this, too: First, recognize personality traits that cause flaws in your behavior; and, second, deal intellectually with subsequent problems they cause.

Too often in golf we divorce ourselves from responsibility for our own golf game by becoming mental nonparticipants. We either settle for less or continually play below our capabilities, or else we totally rely on others to analyze our problems and fix our golf swing for us when things aren't going well.

Although professional expertise and help are always advisable, it also is important for you to know how to help yourself. First understand the basics so you can either improve or correct your own golf swing; and, second, recognize your personal deficiencies and understand how your behavior and mental approach impact your own golf game.

CHAPTER NINE

Emotions
Strong Feelings

A discussion arises periodically among sportsmen and women in general about whether golfers are bona fide athletes or not and, therefore, whether golf should be categorized as a recreation, a sport, or an athletic event. In the final analysis though, whatever it may be, no one can deny that golf as a game, once defined as such, is "an unprecedented emotional experience."

Ask any two golfers who have ever traipsed the fairways in competition about their emotions while playing. Despite the fact that one may have appeared calm in the face of all adversity while the other showed anger and frustration (Illustration 9.1), both are likely to name every emotion from excessive exuberance (A) to club-throwing frustration (B) and describe every emotional feeling that lies in between. Assuming the experience level of the two players was equal, and one displayed excessive emotion while the other did not, who probably won and who probably lost? Undoubtedly the one who maintained composure was the probable winner that day.

Many things influence your emotions, some of which originate from outside yourself, others from within. Outside influences originate from

9.1 Uncontrolled emotion often requires new equipment.

what other people say and do, changes in the weather, conditions on the golf course, and so on. On the other hand, inner emotions stem from what you think about, how you feel, and how you perform—even from how you look if suddenly you feel that absolutely everyone is watching and judging you. Whatever your feelings, however, the challenge is to prevent excessive behavior as a result of any of this.

Although you have little or no control over the occurrence of external influences or distractions, you can learn to become aware of and control your emotions, if not completely, at least to some degree. First, you must recognize the source of the problem, and, second, learn how to cope with your emotions by recognizing and correcting your own shortcomings.

Once you become an established player, often the only difference between being successful or unsuccessful is how you handle yourself on the golf course and how you control your emotions. Things that normally reflect a nice disposition, for instance, such as patience, tolerance, and composure, can quickly ruin a nice golf game if unleashed emotionally as impatience and intolerance due to losing control. Although others may seem to accept bad behavior as just the frustration of golf, these are self-defeating traits in that you are the one who pays with diminished performance for losing control of your emotions.

When not controlled, strong emotions commonly associated with golf that influence one's performance are anger, fear, grief, and joy. Not only are they harmful as isolated emotions that cause quick, instinctive responses, but they cause additional feelings that overcome our physical skills and our ability to perform. For instance, anger causes frustration, fear causes apprehension and loss of confidence, grief causes self-pity and dejection, and uncontrolled joy may cause overconfidence. Take a closer look at these emotions as they relate to golf:

ANGER AND FRUSTRATION

Anger is one of our stronger emotions with a broader spectrum than others, perhaps because the source of anger can be derived at any time from any situation as well as from anything or anyone. If completely uncontrolled in golf, anger so pervades our senses and ability to perform that it quickly joins forces with feelings of frustration. On the other hand, frustration is derived from failure to accomplish what we expect of ourselves: to hit the ball how we want, as far as we want, and exactly where we aim it.

Anger and frustration result from almost anything in golf such as imperfect lies, unlucky bounces, poor results of well-planned shots, bumpy greens, lack of respect by others for *QUIET!* on the golf course, and so on and so forth. Since we've little control over conditions on the course or behavior of other golfers, however, we're better prepared to deal with adverse circumstances when we consistently hit the ball effectively and play the game well.

Simply stated, anger and frustration are caused by hitting poor golf shots that result from a faulty golf swing, proving the point that, as someone once said, "Anger is the result of trying to play hundred-dollar golf shots with a five-dollar swing." Regardless of the circumstances, however, we tend to blame our missed golf shots on anything or anybody except our own shortcomings. So, if you want to hit hundred-dollar golf shots and lessen your frustration, the solution is to curb your anger over adverse situations and redirect your energy toward improving your golf swing.

FEAR AND APPREHENSION

Fear and apprehension, of course, means being afraid. In golf it's being afraid of hitting over water, out of bunkers, under trees, or just flat-out missing golf shots. But fear causes apprehension about making even very makable golf shots, and being apprehensive results in tentative, miss-hit shots that lead to failure and loss of confidence. Fear and lack of confidence result from a poor golf swing that fails to produce successful golf shots; so, if you want to overcome your fear and apprehension, you have to improve your golf swing.

GRIEF

Grief is defined as "deep sadness caused by trouble or loss"—a definition so profound it clearly defines at times the game of golf as well. Certainly we encounter grief when we hit into and out of trouble all day; but grief may quickly turn into anger or destructive self-pity that weakens our ability to meet the challenges of golf.

SELF-PITY

Self-pity is excessiveness in feeling sorry for oneself. In golf it stems from anything that causes pain and anguish: thin fairways, heavy rough, bunkers and barrancas, streams and lakes, inclement weather, and so on. But everyone encounters these. They all are part of the game. The bigger problem lies with what directly affects only you and your golf game: namely, poor golf shots caused by a poor golf swing that result in such dejection and self-pity that you just can't cope with the problems at hand.

If you want to overcome self-pity and dejection, the solution is to improve your golf swing.

JOY

Joy is a strong feeling of pleasure. It is happiness caused by making an impossible golf shot or sinking a sidehill, downhill forty-foot putt. Although no one can be expected to remain completely unemotional during moments like these, you need to be aware that being overly emotional can ruin the rest of your game by causing loss of concentration (i.e., "focus") and by changing timing and rhythm. So how do you overcome the problem of becoming too exuberant? You don't, of course, at least not entirely. Even vast experience can only diminish but never eradicate the sudden joy of thrilling moments in golf. Until you become more experienced, however, and particularly if you play competitively, always enjoy the moment but also be wary of the pitfalls. If you're predisposed to be too emotional, you need only recognize it as a problem with which you may eventually want to deal.

Any emotion displayed in moderation is normal and can be very helpful as an outlet for your feelings. Even becoming angry is normal as long as it stays reasonable and controlled. It's very normal after a really wayward golf shot to show that you care how you play and are only satisfied with your best effort. Many great golfers had terrible tempers as youngsters: swearing, throwing golf clubs, or slamming them into the fairway after a missed golf shot. But uncontrolled temper creates tension and builds pressure whether in competition or when trying only to perform—and pressure leads directly to stress and frustration.

To avoid pressure and think logically and clearly in golf you must adhere to two unwritten rules: (1) play consistently on the same emotional level and (2) never let anything cause you to continually lose control of your emotions. Becoming aware of your emotions and how they affect your play helps you recognize and deal with unwanted emotional upsets that infiltrate your game.

It often takes creative ingenuity to direct your physical skills effectively and prevent your emotions from overpowering your mind. For example, as someone once reported, Walter Hagen, who "carved his name into history with unparalleled professional flair," said that he expected to make at least seven mistakes a round; therefore, when he made a bad shot, it was just one of the seven so he didn't worry about it. By accepting the fact that perfection was unattainable, he found a way to not get upset.

Whatever else golf may be, it also is a recreation and should be played by most players as such. However, when you're not having fun, it helps to remember that playing the course is still a challenge to be met with serious intent. It's a staging area for taming your emotions and honing your skills while *learning* to have fun. Playing in competition also can be fun. Sooner or later you may want to learn to compete effectively, either with partners, against other players, or maybe only against yourself or the golf course, hole by hole, meeting the challenge in search of self-reliance or self-esteem.

When performance is required, golfers are a mixture of those who diligently compete for trophies or for wagers, as opposed to those who still are trying not to be embarrassed off the next tee. Regardless of your progress or your level of expertise, however, always remember this: Controlling your emotions is a factor in your ability to perform.

CHAPTER TEN

Character
Moral Strength
or Weakness

According to history, the game of golf was played in Scotland from the beginning of the fifteenth century. It was forbidden in 1457, however, by an act of the Scottish Parliament when every able-bodied man was required to practice archery, instead of golf, for Scotland's defense of its country.

When golf again became permissible and regained its popularity, both gentility and affluence accompanied the game, dressy attire and etiquette were involved, and golf was reestablished as a gentleman's game (Illustration 10.1). Surely, then, regardless of the difficulty of the course, a gentleman of character and high integrity such as a tam-o'-shantered Scotsman, who felt the harder the struggle the greater the joy of mastery, never, *ever* kicked his "featherie" or guttapercha out of the gorse and heather.

10.1 Character, integrity, and tradition still define "a gentleman's game."

But golf is not easy, nor was it meant to be as introduced by the strong, resourceful Scots. In 1978 Peter Dobereiner wrote of the Scots in his book, *The Glorious World of Golf,* "It is the game of the patient self-reliant man, prepared to meet whatever fortune may befall him."

"As the early Scot found life a hard battle," he wrote, "with good and evil fortune mixed capriciously, and only to be won by patience and steadfastness in adverse circumstances, so in his game he sought to reproduce the greater struggle for the smaller stake. He was in no mind to make the game easier or less trying, but rather sought to increase its natural difficulties, recognizing even in his recreation, that the harder the struggle, the greater was the joy of mastery."

Happily, now we continue the struggle and meet the challenges worldwide as we replicate the links of Scotland that evolved in the sand dunes amidst the gorse and heather. When we duplicate the same formidable adversaries of sand and water, trees and bushes, sloughs and barrancas, rough terrain, hills, and doglegs, we also meet the many challenges of the whimsical nature of golf when the ball bounces into and behind these pits and barriers to readily test our character.

With golf's heritage and tradition founded on such stalwart character as the Scots, it would seem that golfers also inherit an obligation to the game and to its players to respectfully uphold and protect not only one's character but also the tradition of golf as a game of honor and integrity.

RULES, HANDICAPS, AND INTEGRITY

Guided by rules and regulations of the Royal and Ancient Golf Club of St. Andrews, Scotland, and the USGA, the game of golf is watched over by those who continue to respect and protect its values. Along with social golf, this encompasses high-level performance in both professional and amateur competition where rules cannot be changed and are strictly enforced. For example, Rule 1-3 states, "Players must not agree to exclude the operation of any Rule or to waive any penalty incurred"; Rule 9-3 states, "A competitor who has incurred a penalty should inform his marker (scorekeeper) as soon as practicable." As a result of rules like these, as well as tradition, golf is the only game where players call penalties on themselves whether others see a rules infraction or not.

But rules cannot legislate either morality or character. Therefore, unless a golfer is playing at a level of competition where rules are enforced, penalties levied, and players disqualified for improper performance, there occasionally is the tendency to let gain and personal interest override principles.

When a player either drops, replaces, or moves a ball away from where it should be (Illustration 10.2), plays a mulligan here or there, "finds" an obviously lost golf ball, "takes" a missed two-foot putt, or contributes to an incorrect scorecard, it's politely referred to as "an infraction of the rules." And what is gained? A little distance, a better lie, and a more preferred handicap perhaps. Besides outright cheating, though, two things of importance are lost: respect for the game itself and personal integrity, neither of which are worth forfeiting in golf by failure to honor the rules.

But are the rules too stringent or even too self-regulating to support honesty and integrity? Maybe. But then maybe not. Maybe part of the difficulty with compliance originates from within the rules themselves.

The Rules

The regulatory code of the USGA, entitled "The Rules of Golf," requires the ball to be played "as it lies." The only deviation allowed is to play by "winter rules" that may be initiated at individual courses only by The Committee.

In other words, when adverse conditions apply throughout the course, a "local rule" may be posted temporarily to permit lifting, cleaning, and

10.2   . . . but where's the self-esteem and integrity?

replacing the ball within one club-length of where it originally lay, no closer to the hole but in a more preferred place, without penalty. Winter rules are not endorsed by the USGA as an elective for individual players, however, because it permits changing the Rules of Golf to play "preferred lies."

Here's why: When playing under winter rules we learn that under certain inclement circumstances (a) the ball is moveable and (b) we may move it. We also learn that moving off bare lies, from behind trees, out of rough, and so on, makes shots easier and, of course, more fun. So when we're not playing competitively, we often choose, both singly and collectively, to play winter rules (i.e., preferred lies) anytime, anywhere, whether posted or not. And why do we do this? There are two reasons: (1) Partly because playing "vacation golf" is easier, but (2) mostly because golf is a microcosm of life wherein we all have egos that require success and recognition. Moving the ball in golf simply makes us more successful, which is better for our egos.

Although moving the ball is not uncommon when playing "just for fun," and can be helpful by improving confidence, a handicap is required when playing competitively; therefore, if "vacation golf" is played when winter rules are not in effect, but you post the score anyway for handicap purposes, you lose in three ways: (1) you lose the personal challenge of having played with honesty and integrity; (2) you lose the possible satisfaction of having made the impossible golf shot; and (3) if you play in competition you penalize yourself, as well as your partners, by having too low a handicap.

The handicap system in golf is designed to help golfers compete against each other equally on any golf course anywhere. Not only does it require that you play by the rules, it also relies on your posting every score for every game played. In essence, the system can only be as effective as the players for whom it is designed. It doesn't allow for posting only some scores, not posting high scores due to embarrassment, posting only low scores because of pride or ego, or for only posting high scores to maintain a "competitive" handicap.

Because of the importance of the handicap system and the USGA's concern for fairness, there have been extensive changes in the system over the past few years. But the system may also endanger things such as age-old tradition and the spirit of the game, as well as your own integrity, unless you interpret the changes and their intent correctly.

Here's why: Successfully tested in Colorado since 1983, the "Slope System" became the USGA policy for handicapping at the start of 1987, and within this system the USGA employs what is called Equitable Stroke Control—"equitable" meaning fair. Equitable Stroke Control places a ceiling on the score that may be taken on any given hole. For instance, if you have an eighteen handicap, play a difficult par five and shoot a twelve on the hole, you may take only seven, as prescribed, due to your "ceiling." But the system calls for recording that twelve on your scorecard along with (as a suggestion) placing five dots in the box (Illustration 10.3; A). The total dots for eighteen holes are then deducted from your total gross score (B) to determine your adjusted gross score (C). The adjusted score is then posted for your handicap. Although unintended by the USGA, the system also tends to discourage "sandbagging"—the art of manipulating handicaps upward by recording high scores in order to raise a handicap; however, therein lies a problem.

Golf undeniably is a game in which ego is a factor because we measure ourselves by our accomplishments. So here's what happens: Rather than correctly recording a twelve on the hole, common practice is to record a seven and forget the dots, thereby shooting an eighty-nine instead of a ninety-four—and apparently the lower the handicap the more common the practice. "Hey, John, what'd ya shoot today?" "Eighty-nine!" shouts John gleefully, his ego still intact.

Although it may be good for our egos, and it certainly isn't cheating, it does nothing to protect such things as honor or tradition. Just as it puts a

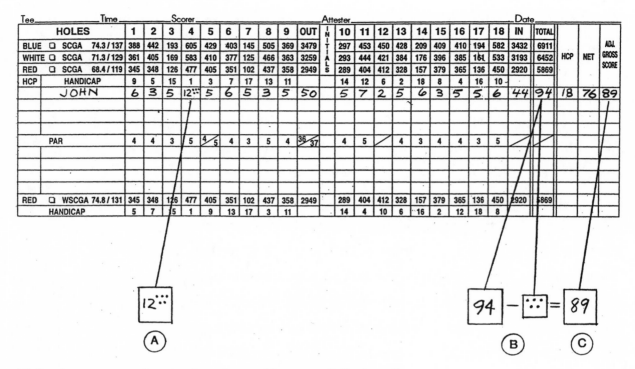

HOLES	1	2	3	4	5	6	7	8	9	OUT	I N I T I A L S	10	11	12	13	14	15	16	17	18	IN	TOTAL		HCP	NET	ADJ. GROSS SCORE
BLUE ☐ SCGA 74.3/137	388	442	193	605	429	403	145	505	369	3479		297	453	450	428	209	409	410	194	582	3432	6911				
WHITE ☐ SCGA 71.3/129	361	405	169	583	410	377	125	466	363	3259		293	444	421	384	176	396	385	161	533	3193	6452		HCP	NET	
RED ☐ SCGA 68.4/119	345	348	126	477	405	351	102	437	358	2949		289	404	412	328	157	379	365	136	450	2920	5869				
HCP HANDICAP	9	5	15	1	3	7	17	13	11			14	12	6	2	18	8	4	16	10						
JOHN	6	3	5	12	5	6	5	3	5	50		5	7	2	5	6	3	5	5	6	44	94		18	76	89
PAR	4	4	3	5	4/5	4	3	5	4	36/37		4	5		4	3	4	4	3	5						
RED ☐ WSCGA 74.8/131	345	348	126	477	405	351	102	437	358	2949		289	404	412	328	157	379	365	136	450	2920	5869				
HANDICAP	5	7	15	1	9	13	17	3	11			14	4	10	6	16	2	12	18	8						

12

(A)

94	−	. .	=	89

(B)   (C)

10.3 Accurate scorekeeping is an honorable responsibility in golf.

ceiling on scoring, it also puts a ceiling on performance because as soon as you reach your "ceiling" on any given hole, you may also stop performing by simply picking up your golf ball and taking the maximum allowed without completing play.

Whatever happened to perseverance and tenacity that provide strength of character and encourage practice, improvement, and gutsy "shotmaking" born of having to finish a botched golf hole? Embarrassment over high scores is what motivates many golfers to want to improve. And what will become of "the patient self-reliant man, prepared to meet whatever fortune may befall him?" When faced with adversity in golf, if nothing else, tradition might suggest that you have an obligation to yourself and to the game to meet the challenge, to try harder, to make the impossible golf shot, to see the game through, and, above all else, to finish the hole. The old clichés apply. As sportswriter Grantland Rice wrote many, many years ago in a poem titled "Alumnus Football," "When the One Great Scorer comes to write against your name, He marks—not that you won or lost—but how you played the game."

Sportsmanship

The game of golf can be diabolically frustrating at times and stories are true of golfers having club-throwing tantrums, breaking shafts, banging heads off drivers, and launching woods and irons into ponds or trees. But the qualities and conduct of a good sportsman—or sportswoman, for that matter—are not only linked to controlling temper and curbing the art form of club throwing. They also include insistence on fair play accompanied by the capacity to win or lose gracefully without arrogance in victory or whining in defeat. With all the pressure involved, understanding the mental aspect of golf is essential to learning to play with any semblance of good sportsmanship.

Along with playing by the rules and maintaining an honest handicap, these forerunners of good sportsmanship also include having a good attitude, an even disposition, emotional self-control, and patience.

Although the majority of golfers, by far, display these attributes and deal with adversity, there still are those who either can't, don't, or won't. But golf is still known as a "gentleman's game" in which things like rules and sportsmanship apply; when we continually abuse the system, we only degrade ourselves.

To play the game fairly you need to play by the rules, score by the rules, and post your scores by the rules because if you forget the spirit of fair play, forfeit character, and overlook tradition, you may win the game you play with others but you miss the challenge of playing with honor and integrity.

PART IV

Results of Meeting the Challenge

CHAPTER ELEVEN

Concentration
Paying Close Attention by Focusing the Mind

Concentration in golf is seldom explained beyond the fact that it is important and should be developed. Beyond that point, the subject remains a true enigma in that you have to consciously think about what you're doing on the one hand, but then not think about it on the other so you can concentrate. The challenge lies in learning how and when to think as well as how and when to concentrate. They are not the same, but both are needed and have their place in golf.

Thinking is defined as "having an idea" or "forming a plan," while *concentration* is defined as "focusing the mind." The two are related in that first you have an idea, thinking, "This is what I'm going to do"; and then your mind starts to concentrate on "This is how I'm going to do it." With knowledge, practice, and experience, concentration eventually becomes the ability to stay focused on the moment while not thinking about what is being done: in essence, being focused without thinking.

In the early stages of learning and practicing basics, golf is estimated to be about ninety percent physical and ten percent mental (Illustration 11.1; A). As one becomes more knowledgeable about swing mechanics, finds

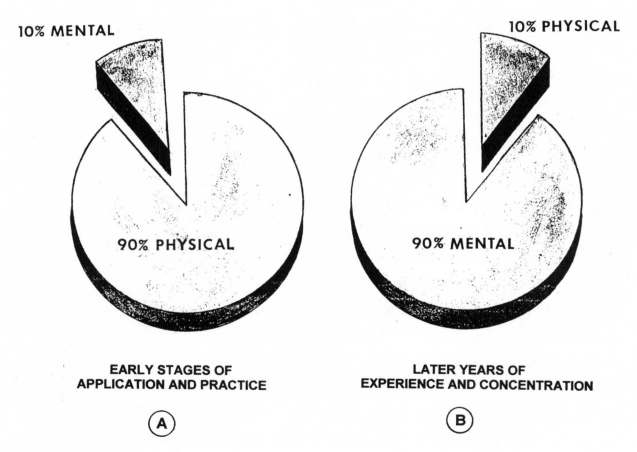

10% MENTAL

90% PHYSICAL

EARLY STAGES OF APPLICATION AND PRACTICE

Ⓐ

10% PHYSICAL

90% MENTAL

LATER YEARS OF EXPERIENCE AND CONCENTRATION

Ⓑ

11.1   This is true!

positions more comfortable and the swing more reliable, however, percentages tend to reverse themselves. Less thinking is needed for implementing basics and more is directed toward making the golf shot, whereupon, of necessity, the percentages reverse themselves as golf becomes more mental and thinking turns to concentration (B).

You have to think about basics when first developing your grip and stance since they are so critically important. In time, however, correctly setting up to the ball becomes more subconscious than conscious, and you start to focus more and more not on *how* but on *where* to hit the golf ball.

The more proficient you become in the application of basics (i.e., fundamentals), the more you free your mind for making golf shots. Consider the prowess of Jack Nicklaus, for example: Having initially learned and practiced basics until he "grooved" his golf swing, early each year thereafter he reviewed these fundamentals with his teacher, Jack Grout, to make certain his swing was mechanically sound. He then trusted those mechanics and clearly played the rest of the year with awesome concentration on the job at hand (Illustration 11.2).

Concentration is the ability to think only about the shot you are making on the hole you are playing—to think less about how you are going to hit the ball and more about where you want to hit it. In golf, what you are able to concentrate on and how you go about it is also important. For instance, learning and practicing your golf swing is how and where you first learn the importance of concentration, and playing is where you recognize the difficulty of maintaining concentration. Maintaining concentration is difficult, however, so getting and keeping it is only part of the challenge.

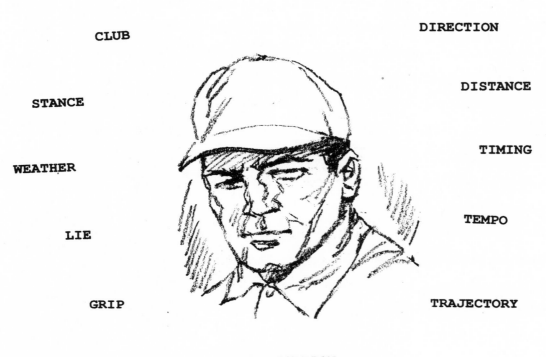

FAIRWAY (PROBLEMS?)

CLUB   DIRECTION

DISTANCE

STANCE

TIMING

WEATHER

TEMPO

LIE

GRIP   TRAJECTORY

APPLICATION

11.2   Concentration requires concentration.

DEVELOPING CONCENTRATION

The ability to concentrate originates from understanding the golf swing, practicing to groove in the basics, and playing and practicing until you can count on results. The more experienced you become at this, the more you learn to concentrate.

Knowledge about requirements for the basic golf swing helps you trust that what you're doing is right, thereby helping you direct your practice and concentration toward making golf shots. The key to concentration is twofold: (1) Practice only one thing at a time and (2) with only a single thought in mind.

Aside from practice, which is where heavy-duty thinking should be done, attempts to think about too many things at the same time creates a muddled image that distracts us from what we should be doing and diminishes our performance, bringing to mind a poem by an unknown poet entitled "The Puzzled Centipede":

> A centipede was happy, quite
> Until a frog in fun
> Said, "Pray, which leg comes after which?"
> This raised her mind to such a pitch
> She lay distracted in the ditch
> Considering how to run.

Conscious attention to an action itself interferes with previously learned automatic response—as noted by the hapless centipede. But the body responds to plans developed prior to an action and doesn't require reminders from conscious thought. Such is the value of knowledge and practice. We learn to do things automatically with continuous movement, such as quickly and accurately set up to the ball and start to swing, without considering the action. Learning should always be directed toward eventually being able to perform an action without mental interference.

With knowledge and practice, conscious thought turns into automatic behavior, whereupon concentration then replaces conscious thought. Concentration can then be used for visualization to create a pre-swing picture with conscious thought now relegated to the use of key swing thoughts—key thoughts being deliberate concentration applied to anything specific that makes the golf swing work.

How well you are able to intermix and balance visualization with key swing thoughts depends on several things: your own proficiency that determines your level of concentration, how well your senses work, and how well you can determine where to best direct your effort. Based on whether you're practicing or playing, what does the shot require? What does your swing require? What are your priorities, goals, objectives, and options? Is "seeing" the landing area as important as feeling where the clubhead is? Is "seeing" the ball sailing around the corner as important as feeling your weight transfer? Can you do both? Maybe. Maybe not.

The key to working out a solution is not to give up one or the other but to use key thoughts in practice to develop your swing in order to minimize their use while playing. That way you can utilize both visual images and key thoughts.

With practice, visual images and key swing thoughts are compatible. You can "see" the ball flying to the target (Illustration 11.3; A), for instance, as you're remembering to turn away from the ball and swing your hands more upright (B). In other words, a sound golf swing and good concentration can handle the thought, "This is what I'm going to do in order to accomplish what I want to do."

Ben Hogan once said, "You have to practice concentration as hard as you practice your golf swing." But concentration is hard work in golf, the difficulty being that for anyone to perform to the best of his or her ability for eighteen holes takes about four hours, a thought so remote that it definitely remains beyond the scope of most golfers—all except Tiger Woods, that is. Along with understanding the importance of concentration,

KEY SWING THOUGHT   **VISUALIZATION**

11.3   Baaaack annnnnd *through*!

it also helps to know how you lose it, how to regain it, and how to keep it once you have it.

LOSS OF CONCENTRATION

Concentration is defined as "focusing the mind." Although we know what it is, why we need it, what it does, and how to get it, what we don't seem to know is how to keep it once we get it; therefore, we lose it in many different ways.

Common things we all fall prey to that disturb our concentration are not necessarily train sounds, sirens, planes, or helicopters, or even barking dogs, squealing tires, or construction noises. Certainly any or all of these may be an annoyance, but they also are normal, predictable, reasonable, familiar, and often continuous, outside distractions with which we all learn to cope. What we don't seem to cope with are the unpredictable, sometimes inconsiderate distractions caused by other golfers: dropping golf bags, rattling clubs, shuffling feet, moving carts, sneezing, talking—or, even worse, whispering. Given time and a backswing that's not too fast, we learn to back away from all of these.

Continuous noises and sudden distractions generally are things over which we have no control. We can learn to tolerate these, however, because we know we need our concentration and we do have control over our feelings and emotions—or should have. Instead of being angry or intolerant, bringing clearly into focus sounds and situations that we know to be distractions helps us maintain or regain our concentration by way of recognition and acceptance.

Although losing concentration can be instantaneous due to sudden distractions or be insidiously pervasive due to someone's inconsiderate talking, loss of concentration is mostly caused by ourselves in several different ways. For instance, we lose concentration through being overly social ourselves, becoming engrossed in another's game, dwelling on a bad shot or bad situation, worrying about winning or losing, playing too slowly, losing composure, or even playing with physical or emotional pain.

Playing Socially

Maintaining concentration is one of the most difficult, yet challenging goals in golf when playing either socially or competitively or a combination of both.

Playing only socially, "just for fun," requires little concentration since little is expected where there is little to accomplish. For serious-minded golfers, though, who combine playing socially with playing competitively, it takes a rare bit of talent to maintain concentration while continually switching from playing the game and making shots to politely trying to listen to what someone is talking about. Yet these are the types of challenges most of us encounter and accept when only playing socially with friends.

Unless you only play competitively, wherein conversation is minimal and the game more serious, you have to learn to deal with interrupted concentration on two levels: First, if you should be the one initiating needless conversation, you either are not the one who wants to play your best or else you have a certain talent for regaining your concentration when it's your turn to play. Also, you not only deny yourself the opportunity to try to do your best by thinking about your next golf shot, but even more importantly you deny other players their right to concentrate.

Second, if you should be the listener, awareness is your best defense. Bring the problem clearly into focus so you can deal with it. It's far, far better—and sometimes easier—to recognize a problem and know how to cope rather than becoming a victim of your own anger and frustration. You can find a way to deal with the problem if you keep your wits about you and maintain your composure.

When you recognize another's enjoyable moment of socializing as a vocal intrusion and a problem for you in golf, use conscious awareness to turn off your concentration on your golf game (which you comfortably can do for a moment or two), recognize and focus clearly on the moment, then turn off your noisy problem by turning on your concentration for your next golf shot. Get a clearcut picture in mind about exactly what you want to do and don't waver from your effort.

Concentration is a skill that must be practiced just as you practice your golf game. Take advantage. Nowhere will you find a better opportunity to practice than when mixing social with competitive golf. As someone once said, "Concentration is the ability to punish yourself for whatever length of time necessary to get the job done."

Becoming Involved in Another's Game

Regardless of the sport, becoming engrossed in another's game when you also are a participant is a primary cause of either having no concentration to begin with or else losing it altogether. Take sailboat racing, for example, as a case in point: In reference to the final windward leg of the penultimate race of the 1973 Swiss Championship, Dr. Stuart H. Walker, author of *Winning: The Psychology of Competition,* described the following incident:

At the leeward mark he had been several hundred yards astern, in about seventh place. I had assumed that the series was in the bag, but now he was coming on strong in the dying air, passing boat after boat. As I looked astern and to leeward, I became mesmerized by his progress. He was pointing higher and footing considerably faster than I, "making land" rapidly. As I calculated the effect of the loss of each boat that he passed, it seemed that I could not take my eyes off him. How could he go so fast when, in the previous races, I had always been faster? What was I doing wrong? How had I trimmed the sails differently? I was, of course, contributing greatly to his progress; not only was he sailing faster in better air, but I, mesmerized by his progress, was slowing my own boat considerably.

Focusing your mind on someone else's boat—or golf game—prevents you from focusing on your own; and the degree to which you help them attain their goals is often the same degree to which you fall short of your own. The time to become involved in someone else's game is only when you have absolutely no aspirations of your own.

Dwelling on a Bad Shot or Bad Situation

Staying too engrossed in your own problems creates even more distractions than being absorbed in another's. Should you dwell on these distractions in the form of bad shots or bad situations, however, you create both anger and frustration, either of which will ruin your performance by wrecking your concentration.

Anger and frustration go hand-in-hand in golf and together result from our own inability to do what we want to do. When the result of our actions is a bad shot, bad lie, or bad bounce on a bad fairway, at first we tend to view results as not our fault but just as bad luck. When it happens repeatedly, we get angry; an inability to prevent "bad luck" creates frustration, which only increases anger.

Anger results from outside sources as well: from players who talk incessantly, give unsolicited lessons, hold up play, disregard or enforce all the rules all the time, and so on. You should be aware that when you become angry at these annoyances, you lose your concentration and composure, and then you lose control.

If you ever have thrown a golf club after hitting a really bad golf shot, you fully understand the nonproductive feeling of completely losing control. In 1922, Seymour Dunn of Scotland wrote in his book, *Golf Fundamentals*, "To allow a trifling misfortune to produce this state of emotion with resulting confusion of thought and unsuccessful body control is to admit weakness of intellect."

Losing control means you are controlled by emotion. When emotions control your thinking, your thoughts become unclear and your attention is no longer focused. Unable to concentrate, you suddenly lack self-confidence and positive thoughts are no longer available to help you execute your next golf shot; so, as Seymour Dunn indicated, it is absolute stupidity to let a bad golf shot or a bad situation result in anger or frustration that ruins your concentration and therefore your golf game.

Worrying about Winning or Losing

According to a study of human nature, all those who compete are not necessarily motivated to win. In fact, the study shows that some people want to lose. Although wanting to lose may be subconscious for some people who either feel they don't deserve to win or find it threatening somehow, most of us really want to win. Meanwhile, there are ways to win and ways to lose but consciously or subconsciously worrying about either while playing is a sure way to lose.

As Grantland Rice's quote is often paraphrased, "It matters not who won or lost, but how you played the game." That may relate to sportsmanship, but when you enter a tournament; have a partner; play for trophies, wagers, or recognition; or play only for the challenge of not beating yourself; winning or losing becomes important in golf. *Worrying* about winning or losing, however, is totally self-defeating.

Worrying about winning or losing stems from thinking about inane things such as how to protect your lead, how much money is at stake, or even how others may judge your performance. Thinking about winning takes your mind off each golf shot and creates fear of losing, while *worrying* about losing causes depression and self-pity that commonly causes losing.

When your mind wanders off to accept trophies and accolades or you start feeling sorry for yourself, you tend to speed up your swing on the one hand and slow down your performance on the other. First you start thinking about scoring instead of making golf shots, then you lose your concentration and then you probably lose the game.

Whatever the circumstances, whether winning or losing, to overcome thinking and worrying about one or the other you have to stay focused on making golf shots: this shot, this hole, this swing, this moment. First you execute each shot to the best of your ability, and then you add your score.

Slow Play

Although slow play on the golf course certainly is a problem, it is interesting to note that the golfer who acknowledges being part of the problem is yet to be found. Slow play is *always* caused by "others" and nothing speeds "them" up.

The truth is, however, that players simply playing and doing things too slowly create the problem; therefore, either helping to overcome or else accept slow play requires an awareness of what others do as well as a recognition of our own deficiencies regarding any number of things:

1. Not being in the right place at the right time when it's your turn to hit.
2. Parking bags and carts in the wrong place.
3. Retrieving clubs left behind.
4. Taking too long to assess the shot.
5. Indecision about club selection.
6. Taking too many practice swings.
7. Standing over the ball too long for any reason while getting ready to hit.
8. Looking up rules on the tee or not hitting a "provisional" if playing by the rules.
9. Replacing clubs in the bag upon leaving the green instead of replacing them at the next tee.
10. Hitting into trouble and searching "overtime."

Since "taking too long" in golf has no clock time except as required for certain tournament play, *exactly* how long is not the point. "Too long" simply means going beyond what is reasonable.

Taking too long to actually hit the ball more often than not results from either fear in lieu of confidence or from not knowing what to do or how to go about it. When you do know what to do, however, fear is not a factor and you step right up and get right to it before you lose your concentration. Your nervous system isn't meant to cope with the strain of prolonged fixed attention; therefore, concentration comes and goes to protect your nervous system. Nerves can't cope with several seconds of decision-making, several more for preparation, and yet even more for just staring at the golf ball. You lose your concentration to protect your nervous system. In psychology this is known as the "automatic cut-out of the attention system."

William James, an American psychologist and philosopher, wrote, "There is no such thing as voluntary attention for more than a few seconds at a time." By way of proving this he used an illustration of a two-inch square inside of and connected at the corners with a four-inch square. As one studies the illustration, the inside square appears to move from background to foreground, then shifts back again, each change demonstrating a break in one's attention span. On the average, experts have determined that this break in concentration occurs about every three seconds. Because a person's concentration breaks so often within a given time, slower play results in worse play.

Because of the attention factor which, granted, may be a shade longer for some than others, taking too long to make the shot once you are mentally prepared results in mistakes because it affects coordination. Consider this, for instance: Just as anger and frustration go hand-in-hand while playing, concentration and coordination go hand-in-hand when making a golf shot. For example, picture yourself throwing a rock through a window. You see the window as the target, you concentrate on throwing the rock, and you "pull the trigger" mentally as your arm draws back to throw and your whole body responds automatically. That's concentration and coordination. The same is true in golf.

As your mind gets ready to make the shot, your body gets ready, too; but when you don't "pull the trigger" when first ready, your concentration quick-changes from "seeing" the landing area as the target to seeing the ball instead. Since hitting the ball is, after all, a real objective in golf, suddenly there is a spontaneous, all-out effort made to hit the ball as the target rather than hitting it to a landing area. This not only affects coordination but also affects hitting the ball.

Slow play is caused by all of us who fail to recognize ourselves as part of the problem. But you also contribute to slow play when you make mistakes, hit too many golf shots, and have to look for lost golf balls—partly because you lost your concentration at address when you took too long and caused slow play. The way to play better is to play faster by speeding up preparation; and the way to play faster is to play better through know-how and practice.

Playing with Pain

Everyone encounters pain from time to time, both physical and emotional, and learning how to deal with it is difficult.

Since every physical pain encountered is not a serious problem, nor can pain always be eliminated, many spunky golfers routinely learn to play with pain by being willing to accept a lower performance level. Those unaccustomed to playing with pain, though, generally cannot; so, rather than choosing to lower their performance level, they may continue trying to play at peak level.

Assuredly some people have more tolerance to pain than others and can "bite the bullet," override the pain, and successfully carry on as usual—up to a point. Many others, however, continue to play with golf-related injuries that not only ruin their immediate performance but often also ruin months, or even years, of still enjoyable golf.

For reasons known only to golfers, many try to work around an injury by every conceivable method known except quitting for awhile—even to the point of making up a different golf swing every other hole or so, trying to circumvent the pain. The result of compensation, of course, is that you jeopardize your own golf swing when the others won't work. Just as you can't overcome problems created by a poor golf swing, neither can your golf swing overcome problems created by pain.

Your body will neither shift its weight nor turn around or against a painful obstacle such as a foot that needs repair, a knee or hip that may need replacement, a shoulder that needs surgery, or a back that needs time off to heal. The body stops performing and starts to protect itself by using pain as its protector. Yet the very core of success in golf is shifting your weight and turning; so, when you try to do what you can't do (just because you used to) the result is loss of concentration, anger and frustration, and undoubtedly a far-below-expectations golf game. There comes a time for everyone when it's only sensible to recognize when you can't handle pain—either physically or emotionally—and, even if begrudgingly, just give it up for a while.

The average tour player is purported to sustain at least two serious injuries throughout his or her career, the most serious affecting the lower back, left wrist, left knee, and left shoulder. Other players sustain these injuries also, but tour players who equate playing well with feeling well are prone to just "hang it up" a while within the time allotted by their doctor, or else they get the medical problem fixed—and you should, too.

You have to recognize in golf that when persistent pain exists you absolutely cannot perform to the best of your ability. Generally this causes other problems and everything gets worse. So recognize a problem early and get it fixed. Given time, almost any body part will either repair itself through inactivity or can be repaired or replaced by competent doctors and good treatment. Your health and disposition will improve, which improves concentration and your golf swing, too.

Losing Your Composure

Due to our own emotional makeup and temperament, few of us can prevent having mood swings that affect our concentration at times. Aside from outside disturbances, we also encounter our own golf shots that are fairly awesome at times. Remember that a great golf shot can be just as disruptive as our worst shot and become a distraction from hitting the next shot. One of the greatest challenges we face in golf is accepting the bad with the good—*and* the good with the bad—by keeping our composure.

Composure is defined as "calmness; quietness; serenity; tranquility"— none of which realistically describe one's ongoing attitude or feelings throughout a round of golf. Yet composure is essential to maintaining control. In essence, maintaining your composure is nothing more than self-control that makes available to you all the other things that help you "smell the roses," so to speak, during your "walk in the park."

Losing your composure makes you lose your concentration, thereby letting only your emotions control your behavior. There may be a reason, though, found in the theory that "when a man of strong character leaves his element, he's often a weaker man." He may be totally in command and at ease in his own bailiwick but feel out of place, embarrassed, and self-conscious when he is outside his element on a golf course, thereby losing composure.

Very few golfers who fail to develop an on-course attitude of composure, however, ever attain their own potential when they sacrifice this self-control. These are the club-throwers and sulkers who cuss out themselves, their surroundings, and all their circumstances. They expect perfection where there is none and lack the ability to come to terms with frustration. On the other hand, those with composure are able to accept the unpredictable, take it all in stride, and be that much stronger for their effort.

Remember the old adage mentioned in chapter 7: "Hope for the best, prepare for the worst, and take whatever comes with a smile." This certainly applies in golf, for you're a winner anywhere if you just don't beat yourself by losing your composure.

MAINTAINING OR REGAINING CONCENTRATION

If you are looking for proficiency in golf, you need to recognize that concentration is elusive and difficult so you can work even harder to develop and preserve it. You may not be able to play like a pro, but you can learn to concentrate like one by learning how to keep it once you have it.

Whether practicing or playing, it is so important to your game that it is worth striving for.

Often the hardest part of concentration is keeping it long enough to implement a pre-planned action. Even though you may be experienced in pre-swing action, you still may lose it periodically (Illustration 11.4): You look down the fairway to "sight" the target (A); waggle a bit to "feel" the swing (B); glance back at the target to "see" the shot (C); start to swing and—"Poof!"—it's gone (D)! Even professionals occasionally stop and start again because they lose their concentration; but the more you know and practice, the less frequently it happens.

Professionals manage their concentration in different ways. Some converse with each other or the gallery, others don't; some are bothered by distractions, others aren't; some submit to "fairway interviews," others won't. What they all have learned and have in common regardless of what they do, however, is either to cope with or avoid anything that disrupts their concentration, and to recover their concentration by the time it's their turn to hit. Whatever your situation may be at any given time, that's the key: It is okay to lose concentration if you quickly can restore it when it is your turn to hit.

Terms used by professionals with regard to concentration are enlightening and, once understood, can be helpful to you. Some refer to being "in the zone," others to "being focused." Once questioned about his deliberate procedure on every shot, Jack Nicklaus referred to it as "waiting for a sense of readiness." The terms themselves are interesting because they divulge a very slight difference between thinking and concentrating. Being "in the zone" throughout a round and "being focused" for eighteen holes are similar in implication but not in application.

POOF

11.4 Oh, well. Restart the engines.

For instance, you can be "in the zone" for eighteen holes because the word "zone" means "a definite region or area." In golf this means keeping your mind on your golf game for eighteen holes by not letting your thinking stray beyond golf. Because your nervous system cannot endure sustained concentration for more than several seconds, however, much less for an entire round, "being focused" with intense concentration for that same amount of time is hardly feasible.

Thinking, remember, is having an idea or forming a plan. On the other hand, concentration is focusing the mind. In other words, you can be "in the zone" for eighteen holes by keeping your thinking within the realm of playing the game while also "being focused"—or reserving your concentration—specifically for each golf shot. Essentially this is what Jack Nicklaus meant. While keeping his mind on playing the game and playing the course he reserved his "sense of readiness" for each golf shot.

The kind of concentration needed for playing well, making shots, reaching goals, and being proud of yourself is not easy. Indeed, it is difficult since being able to concentrate on whatever is needed to make the shots results from knowing how and where to apply your thinking even before you step up to the ball. It only comes with learning everything you can about the game and yourself, as well as with lots of practice.

The more you understand what to do and how to go about it, the more you meet the challenge of learning to play better while enjoying the game more.

CHAPTER TWELVE

Confidence
A Firm Belief in Oneself and One's Abilities

Because of the difficulty and time-consuming effort needed for learning to play golf, rather than facing the task of learning to play well, many players find it easier to accept mediocrity and settle for playing below their own proficiency level. Rather than building confidence in their ability, far too often golfers accept the "I can't" philosophy before meeting the challenge of learning to play better.

Confidence is a belief in yourself: a realistic faith that whatever it is, you can make it happen, fulfill the dream, and reach the goal. It's feeling sure of your ability to do something. But confidence in one's ability is hard-earned and takes patience. Learning positions and swing mechanics often seems easy compared with the time it takes to smooth it all together and play consistently well with confidence. While reaching this plateau, however, confidence continues to grow and develop as long as you continue to develop your golf game with a positive attitude.

As you develop confidence in both yourself and your game, knowing you can do it gives you courage to try. As a result, when you have ability and think you can make a good shot, you usually can. And what if you don't have confidence? It would have been far better had you developed the confidence and missed because you tried. Having confidence does not ensure winning or even making the golf shot; it ensures only that you do your best. Missing shots and making mistakes should only encourage you to move forward with expectation of accomplishment. Trying and missing only points out weakness—not failure—giving you the opportunity to strengthen that part of your game by learning more about it and by practicing.

Whether learning, practicing, or playing golf, the mental aspect of the game constantly pits the power of positive thoughts against the power of negative thoughts, continually forcing a choice between "I can do it" and "I can't." The first instills confidence; however, the second instills only self-defeating negativism. So it definitely helps to stay up and be positive about every aspect of golf.

Although confidence is enhanced by a favorable perception of one's ability, it also must have validity because the power of positive thinking is only as great as it is realistic. This is why staying with the game long enough to develop confidence in your ability is important to eliminate negativism by giving you self-assurance. Eventually you won't just think you can do it— whatever "it" may be; you will know you can through experience. When faced with hitting around, over, or out of trouble, "I can do it" then becomes reality.

Golf is a challenge not meant to expose your weaknesses but to help you find your strengths. It is the challenge of overcoming fear, anxiety, tension, and pressure with knowledge and practice. Playing well is not accidental. You make it happen with actions and decisions that result in skill and experience. Meeting the challenge builds confidence—and it takes a lot of confidence to meet the challenge of playing well.

DEVELOPING CONFIDENCE

Confidence results from developing your abilities while at the same time discovering and accepting your limitations. Trying to do things beyond your capability only creates frustration and tension that prevents your playing as well as you can. If you haven't yet learned to intentionally hook or slice the ball, don't try while playing, but do try to master it on the driving range. Try to determine how well you can play and then, at the level where you play your best, strive for—but don't expect—perfection. Also, since no one plays at peak performance all the time, be prepared to settle for less, which is how you maintain confidence.

Playing as well as you can at any level of proficiency includes setting up with a repeatable pre-shot routine based on sound objectives—something you're able to count on all the time. Once you become an established golfer, confidence results from having trust in what you're doing: making the right club selection, knowing the golf course, using good course management, being able to read the greens, and so on. Along with experience in all these things, confidence develops through continuing to practice your set-up and your golf swing. On the practice range you develop your golf swing (Illustration 12.1; A). On the course you apply what you've developed—including confidence (B).

12.1 Practice confidence.

As you progress in golf and gain more confidence, tournament play and competitive situations inspire you to play better. The more you put yourself in these situations, whether you win or lose, the more you learn to handle them with confidence. Learning how to win includes learning how to lose because in losing you create a strong desire to try harder to win.

Confidence in competition develops from playing practice rounds where you continually deal with all the subtleties and variables of things like types of lies; high and low shots; depth and texture of fairways and rough, as well as moisture conditions; conformation of the course and greens; and flagstick positions. Playing difficult shots in practice rounds, as well as playing the ball "as it lies," makes you better prepared to play these shots when you have to. The better you prepare for anything, the higher your level of confidence.

LOSS OF CONFIDENCE

Regardless of ability, experience, or circumstance, loss of confidence is apt to plague even the best of golfers at times. Although some might call it "nervousness" and others call it "choking," neither defines the problem because losing confidence is due to pressure brought on by various circumstances. But then pressure on the golf course and learning how to deal with it are also part of golf.

Both pressure and a resultant loss of confidence are caused by any number of things that cause both fear and apprehension: fear of failure; fear of embarrassment; fear of hitting a certain golf club; fear of missing the shot; fear of letting your partner(s) down; fear of losing money, the game, match, or tournament, and often even friendships! Regardless of the source of pressure, however, the bottom line is this: Pressure is caused by fear of missing golf shots and is completely self-induced.

Fear and loss of confidence are part and parcel of the same thing: One causes the other. When you are afraid of missing your shot for any pressure-packed reason you become afraid to hit the golf ball. You either decelerate and quit on the shot or else swing too fast to hurry and get it over with, either of which ruin your timing and coordination—and probably your disposition and golf shot, as well.

Many golf shots are hard to make. It is only natural to lack confidence in your ability to hit out of a divot, hit short shots over a hazard or off thin lies, rip the golf ball out of heavy rough, and so on. These shots are difficult for everyone. The challenge is to keep your wits about you, concentrate on making the best shot you can, keep your composure, and try to maintain your confidence. Without confidence you play badly—and when you play badly you lose your confidence. At any level of play, therefore, maintaining confidence is vital to the cause.

MAINTAINING OR REGAINING CONFIDENCE

Being confident denotes success: winning rather than losing, being first instead of last, attaining goals rather than failing, knowing you can win, knowing you can make the shot. Once developed, however, maintaining confidence depends on continuing to practice while expanding on knowledge and experience. You cannot learn too much about the golf swing. Neither can you gain too much experience, nor practice too much. This is how you maintain confidence in your ability, how you overcome pressure and fear.

Knowledge about the golf swing helps you learn about prevention and correction of swing problems as well as what causes bad shots and what you need to practice to turn them into good shots. Unless you are able to recognize and fix the weak parts of your game, the areas in which you have the least confidence tend to break down first under pressure and eventually affect the others.

Winning in golf requires hitting more good shots than bad; so, reaffirm your ability by practicing shots you are sure of. Also practice shots in which you have no confidence, such as hitting over hazards or under trees—and especially practice chipping and putting; then, when you encounter these shots, they seem less intimidating.

Try a little imagination to conjure up hazards and practice being successful. When you see yourself as successful, you see yourself as a winner (Illustration 12.2). There is absolutely nothing wrong with a little déjà vu when playing to help you with your confidence.

12.2 See there? You did it!

You have to be your own person when you play golf. Don't be lured into taking unnecessary risks by trying to do what someone else has done. Play with better players for experience, but if they cut corners and you can't, continue to play within yourself. To maintain confidence, you have to learn to like what you do and trust yourself because of what you do. Bring every situation down to the reality of what you can do to the best of your ability, and you'll be the confident golfer you want to be *because* you've met the challenge.

Index